MESA VERDE
ANCIENT ARCHITECTURE

Avanyu Publishing Inc.®

MESA VERDE
ANCIENT ARCHITECTURE

by Jesse Walter Fewkes

Introduction by Larry V. Nordby, Research Archaeologist, Mesa Verde National Park

Selections from the Smithsonian Institution,Bureau of American Ethnology, Bulletins 41 and 51 from the years 1909 and 1911

Avanyu Publishing Inc.®

© New material
Avanyu Publishing Inc., 1999

ISBN 0-936755-23-7

Library of Congress Cataloging-in-Publication data

Fewkes, Jesse Walter, 1850-1930.
  Mesa Verde ancient architecture : selections from the
Smithsonian Institution, Bureau of American Ethnology,
Bulletins 41 and 51 from the years 1909 and 1911 / by Jesse
Walter Fewkes ; introduction by Larry V. Nordby.
      p.   cm.
    ISBN 0-936755-23-7
    1. Pueblo architecture--Colorado--Mesa Verde National Park.
2. Cliff-dwellings-- Colorado--Mesa Verde National Park. 3.
Pueblo Indians--Dwellings--Colorado--Mesa Verde National
Park. 4. Mesa Verde National Park (Colo.)--Antiquities. I. Title.
E99.P9F42   1999   99-14433
978.8'27--dc21   CIP

Printed in United States of America
First Printing 1999

Cover is Plate 2, 1911 BAE.
Back cover quote from "A Social Divide Written in Stone," by David
Roberts, Smithsonian Magazine, February, 1999.
Backcover photo of Jesse W. Fewkes standing in front of the first
museum at Mesa Verde National Park. Courtesy Mesa Verde
National Park

Table of Contents

Introduction by Larry V. Nordby

Introduction

In many ways, the turn-of-the-century work of J.W. Fewkes at the new Mesa Verde National Park set the stage for what was then regarded as archaeology. Fewkes efforts were designed to publicize these great ruins of the Southwest to the people of the nation, who might then be enticed to visit the Park. Cliff dwellings like Spruce Tree House and Cliff Palace were spectacularly preserved, and a major thrust of Fewkes' excavations was to permit a safe visit and to stabilize or preserve the sites.

Understanding what life was like in these places was related to clearing away the rubble to expose the individual rooms and the overall ground plan of each. As he did so, Jesse Fewkes took notes on the various rooms and kivas, occasionally commenting on what he found that was unusual about each one. Most often, these observations are limited to architecture or its condition. For example, commenting on Room 2 at Spruce Tree House, Fewkes noted that:

> *"This room possesses a feature which is unique. The base of its south wall is supported by curved timbers, whose ends rest on walls, while the middle is supported by a pillar of masonry."*

This unusual piece of construction remains standing today.

While working as an ethnologist, Fewkes had also visited a number of pueblos, describing some of the social and ceremonial life that he observed. This led him to "re-populate" these ancient sites with modern-day descendants, who were doing some of the things that he had observed. Many observations are tied to how small room features such as grinding bins were used, but sometimes Fewkes' descriptions of room use are couched in language that leads the reader in directions that he must have wished to take them. For example, referring to Rooms 71-74, and 79-80 at Cliff Palace he defined, "what is here arbitrarily designated Speaker-chief's House...." A few sentences later he refers to an elaborate banquette that "probably was designed for the use of the Speaker-chief...." These ethnological transformations are the source of many criticisms of Fewkes' work, both among his contemporaries and when viewed in the rear view mirror of current archaeologists.

Revisiting the Sites

The two cliff dwellings described in Fewkes' reports were revisited during the 1930s by the Civil Conservation Corps, who mapped the sites in much greater detail than Fewkes had done. These maps retained the same numbering systems that Fewkes had introduced, but individual rooms and kivas at Cliff Palace were drawn at a much larger scale. At Spruce Tree House, crews led by architects drew basic elevations that showed overall wall form and outline, along with the positions of the doorways.

Photography was a favored medium for recording walls, especially when new stabilization work was done or planned. These photographs would generally depict the map reference points, and ropes were positioned to demarcate those areas that were repaired by Fewkes or CCC crews, so that they would not be confused with the areas of original masonry. Legends of Southwestern archaeology such as Earl Morris and Al Lancaster directed these projects, and Albuquerque architect Stanley Morse was responsible for mapping.

The map of Cliff Palace made by Morse is among the most significant contributions to the archaeology of the site. He prepared his map as a series of sheets, with a scale of about two feet per inch. The result was a set of ten or twelve sheets showing a great deal of detail. These sheets were too cumbersome for field work however. He mapped not only the base of the walls, but also the tops. Many of the walls were out of plumb or thicker at the base, inherently unstable conditions. All doorways were plotted, as were larger wall pegs and remnant roofing beams. None of this information was available from working with Fewkes' materials.

During this same period, two major contributions were the stabilization of the Speaker Chief's House, built atop a huge boulder that was slowly sliding out of the alcove, and the stabilization of the four storey tower (Fewkes' Room 11) within Cliff Palace. The area below the former structure was stabilized by clearing the unconsolidated deposits to bedrock and placing tons of concrete and a series of screw jacks to support the boulder. Then Lancaster built a modern masonry wall to obscure the cement and jacks.

The four-storey tower contained unique white plaster and red painted design throughout its entire height, but was unfortunately missing the northwestern corner from top to bottom. Lancaster rebuilt it, completing the job so skillfully that the modern replacement work blends with workmanship from 700 years earlier. The interior plaster repair is flawless, and all exterior cement joint work was overpointed with soil mortar.

Although emphasizing work that was done at Cliff Palace, the preceding discussion exemplifies the focus that dominated archaeological approaches throughout Mesa Verde National Park since Fewkes did his work: site preservation and meeting the public's demand for visiting such places. Not much additional archaeological research on these sites transpired until the 1990s, when dendrochronological* work was renewed at several cliff sites, including Spruce Tree House and Cliff Palace. Although it was known that the cliff sites were built predominantly during the A.D. 1200s, this work helped to understand more about how the sites grew throughout that century. Essentially, the question is one of determining individual site histories. For this we will turn to Cliff Palace, where the most intensive work has been done during the past decade.

---

*"dendrochronology" is the science of dating past events by a comparative study of growth rings in tree trunks." Webster's New World Dictionary.

Cliff Palace Revisited

In 1995, water seepage in the rear of Cliff Palace introduced a preservation problem to portions of the site, mostly in the rooms around Kivas J and M (Fewkes' map). This water was entering the site through pore spaces in the bedrock, an event that would be impossible to stop. Original mortar loss and plaster exfoliation were the two major kinds of damage anticipated, so these areas were scheduled for intensive documentation before there were more damage. Building on this success, additional monies were obtained to support data compilation over the entire site. Documentation has been ongoing since then, and during 1999 the work will be completed. MVNP has obtained money to carry out a similar project at Spruce Tree House, beginning in AD 2000.

The research template for these architectural archaeology projects is expressed as a hierarchical model that starts with the study of very rudimentary construction materials. Once that has been completed, the model evaluates more complex architectural units such as walls, rooms, room suites, courtyard complexes, dual divisions, the village, and the community of sites that extends beyond the boundaries of Cliff Palace. The combinations and recombinations of these various analytical units supplies a very powerful interpretive tool for revisiting and testing some of Fewkes' observations, including some of his less colorful ones about social and ceremonial interactions. At the same time, it helps to ensure data comparability between structures, something that is difficult to extract from Fewkes' often anecdotal descriptions.

To apply this template at Cliff Palace requires several things that Fewkes lacked. The first is nearly a century of observations by a phalanx of professionals on how to interpret archaeological data. These data are often qualitative and at least partially subjective, and are generally drawn from archaeological sites that were unknown to him. The next is computer technology. It is now much easier to collect graphic data with better and faster camera equipment than Fewkes probably ever imagined.

We have structured the series of architectural and archaeological observations into a database that consists of two parts. Written in Access 97, this database, called ArkDoc, consists of about 230 fields of descriptive data on wall, floor, and roof construction methods. These data are recorded for each room or kiva. The database also includes information on the condition of each room or kiva in an additional 50 fields of data, and contains about the same number of fields concerning dendrochronological data. Altogether, this information comprises a tabular or listed set of information that can be linked to maps of individual rooms, which is a portion of the graphic part of the database.

Each room or kiva has a digital map crafted from the work of architect Morse in the 1930s, to which the locations of stabilization work done by Lancaster's stonemasons has been added. Incorporating Fewkes' room numbering system whenever possible, a new numbering system allows each architectural space to be tracked through the database. Tree ring data are marked on the map, and a rough construction sequence has been established for the entire village. .

Each wall has been photographed, both to create a baseline condition, and to show the kinds and frequency of wall features that Fewkes' maps were too small to show. These photographs have been used to create electronic elevational drawings of each wall, with the features added to the elevations and cross-checked against the map. The designators that can be used to track the distributions of such features as T-shaped doorways or wall pegs, or dated tree-ring specimens are shown on the drawings and the maps. Dimensions have been recorded in the database, and the values for each room are displayed when one "clicks" with a mouse on the graphics depicting that room. These data have allowed us to apply developments of a century of archaeological method and theory to Cliff Palace.

While this introduction to Fewkes' contributions to work at two major sites at Mesa Verde does not permit detailed information on what we have learned about Cliff Palace since he worked here, we can summarize some of the recent findings.

Fewkes' tally of about 95 rooms should be increased to about 150 rooms. We enumerated these rooms differently than he did. We also spent time atop the ledge, counting rooms there. There are about nine additional rooms there, which have now been mapped and documented.

There are about 75 additional open spaces (rooftop plazas, kiva top courtyards, and terraces) that were used differently than enclosed rooms, but were an important part of village life.

Of the 23 kivas that Fewkes numbered, probably two structures, Kivas O and R, never served as kivas. They may be unfinished kivas, but it is likely that they are some other kind of social gathering space that was left unroofed. Fewkes recognized that these structures were different than the other kivas at Cliff Palace. There was also at least one other kiva that was filled and the space reused by Kiva J. The site contains a number of non-family spaces. These probably include the two large rooms in the middle of the site (Rooms 59 and 64), at least a portion of the Speaker Chief complex, Kiva W, and the kivas linked at the southern end of the site: Kivas A, B, and D.

Three of the rooms on the ledge are probably related to community storage for units larger than the family; these rooms were accessed from the roof of Room 68.

Based on the relative rarity of living rooms, which once had hearths, only about 25 households or families lived in Cliff Palace, probably a population of about 100-120 residents. These people may have served as a caretaking population for the site, which may have been visited by much larger numbers of people at special times of year. This would explain why there are large numbers of storage rooms and kivas.

Previously, the site had such a small number of tree-ring dated units that little was known about the construction history. Construction phases begin about AD 1190-1191 (the Kiva F area), followed by a major building episode that occurred about AD 1240-1244 (the area between the Speaker Chief Complex and Rooms 39 and 40); and an expansion toward the south that involved remodeling of some parts of the site and occurred between AD 1268-1274 (Kivas L, M, and N ranging southward to Kiva E).

The last construction episode is dated to AD 1278-1280; it involved Kivas O and R. These buildings are part of a dual division that is represented by Rooms 59 and 64. In particular, Room 59 is associated with Kiva O and Room 64 is linked to Kiva R. The wall immediately south of Kiva R helps to divide the site into two parts of unequal size. Rooms 57 and 58 are approximately on this dividing line, and rooms on the ledge mirror this division. The Speaker Chief Complex was probably in place prior to AD 1264, and may later have been used to articulate the two dual divisions into a single village, along with Kiva Q. Plaster details in this kiva indicate that it was painted symmetrically.

This brief summary demonstrates that what Fewkes began with his allegations about relationships between the pueblo people of his day and their ancestral buildings continues to be of interest to archaeologists today. In the months and years ahead, comparisons between his observations and modern findings will abound. I wonder what Fewkes would think if he knew he was creating the standard for comparison with archaeologists working almost 100 years later.

Larry V. Nordby

Research Archaeologist

Mesa Verde National Park

SMITHSONIAN INSTITUTION
BUREAU OF AMERICAN ETHNOLOGY
BULLETIN 41

ANTIQUITIES OF THE MESA VERDE NATIONAL PÁRK

SPRUCE-TREE HOUSE

BY

JESSE WALTER FEWKES

WASHINGTON
GOVERNMENT PRINTING OFFICE
1909

LETTER OF TRANSMITTAL

SMITHSONIAN INSTITUTION,
BUREAU OF AMERICAN ETHNOLOGY,
Washington, D. C., January 4, 1909.

SIR: I have the honor to submit herewith for publication, with your approval, as Bulletin 41 of this Bureau, the report of Dr. Jesse Walter Fewkes on the work of excavation and repair of Spruce-tree cliff-ruin in the Mesa Verde National Park, Colorado. This was undertaken, pursuant to your instructions, under the direction of the Secretary of the Interior, and a résumé of the general results accomplished is published in the latter's annual report for 1907–8. The present paper is more detailed, and deals with the technical archeological results.

It is gratifying to state that Doctor Fewkes was able to complete the work assigned him, and that Spruce-tree House—the largest ruin in Mesa Verde Park with the exception of the Cliff Palace—is now accessible for the first time, in all its features, to those who would view one of the great aboriginal monuments of our country. This is the more important since Spruce-tree House fulfills the requirements of a "type ruin," and since, owing to its situation, it is the cliff-dwelling from which most tourists obtain their first impressions of structures of this character.

Respectfully, yours,   W. H. HOLMES, *Chief.*

The SECRETARY OF THE SMITHSONIAN INSTITUTION,
Washington, D. C.

CONTENTS

ILLUSTRATIONS

ANTIQUITIES OF THE MESA VERDE NATIONAL PARK

SPRUCE-TREE HOUSE

By Jesse Walter Fewkes

SITE OF THE RUIN

Spruce-tree House (pls. 1, 2)[a] is situated in the eastern side of Spruce-tree canyon, a spur of Navaho canyon, which at the site of the ruin is about 150 feet deep, with precipitous walls. The canyon ends blindly at the northern extremity, where there is a spring of good water; it is wooded with tall piñons, cedars, and stately spruces, the tops of which in some cases reach from its bed to its rim. The trees predominating on the rim of the canyon are cedars and pines.

The rock out of which the canyon is eroded is sandstone of varying degrees of hardness alternating with layers of coal and shale. The water percolating through this sandstone, on meeting the harder shale, seeps out of the cliffs to the surface. As the water permeates the rock it gradually undermines the harder layers of sandstone, which fall in great blocks, often leaving arches of rock above deep caves. One of these caves is situated at the end of the canyon where the rim rock overhangs the spring, which is filled by water seeping down from above the shale. Another of these caves is that in which Spruce-tree House is situated. Several smaller caves, and ledges of rock harder than that immediately above, serve as sites for small buildings.

The wearing away of the fallen fragments of the cliffs is much hastened by the waterfalls which in time of heavy rains fall over the rim rock, their force being greatly augmented by the height from which the water is precipitated. The fragments continually falling from the roofs of the caves form a talus that extends from the floors of the caves down the side of the cliff. The cliff-dwellings are erected on the top of this talus.

---

[a] The photographs from which plates 2–4, 6, 8–14 were made were taken by Mr. J. Nussbaum, photographer of the Archæological Institute of America.

RECENT HISTORY

Although there was once an old Spanish trail winding over the mountains by way of Mancos and Dolores from what is now New Mexico to Utah, the early visitors to this part of Colorado seem not to have been impressed with the prehistoric cliff-houses in the Montezuma valley and on the Mesa Verde; at least they left no accounts of them in their writings. It appears that these early Spanish travelers encountered the Ute, possibly the Navaho Indians, along this trail, but the more peaceable people who built and occupied the villages now ruins in the neighborhood of Mancos and Cortez had apparently disappeared even at that early date. Indian legends regarding the inhabitants of the cliff-dwellings of the Mesa Verde are very limited and indistinct. The Ute designate them as the houses of the dead, or *moki*, the name commonly applied to the Hopi of Arizona. One of the Ute legends mentions the last battle between the ancient house-builders of Montezuma valley and their ancestors, near Battle Rock, in which it is said that the former were defeated and turned into fishes.

The ruins in Mancos canyon were discovered and first explored in 1874 by a Government party under Mr. W. H. Jackson.[a] The walls of ruins situated in the valley have been so long exposed to the weather that they are very much broken down, being practically nothing more than mounds. The few cliff-dwellings in Mancos canyon which were examined by Jackson are for the most part small; these are found on the west side. One of the largest is now known as Jackson ruin.

In the year 1875 Prof. W. H. Holmes, now Chief of the Bureau of American Ethnology, made a trip through Mancos canyon and examined several ruins. He described and figured several cliff-houses overlooked by Jackson and drew attention to the remarkable stone towers which are so characteristic of this region.[b] Professor Holmes secured a small collection of earthenware vessels, generally fragmentary, and also a few objects of shells, bone, and wood, figures and descriptions of which accompany his report. Neither Jackson nor Holmes, however, saw the most magnificent ruins of the Mesa Verde. Had they followed up the side canyon of the Mancos they would have discovered, as stated by Nordenskiöld, " ruins so magnificent that they surpass anything of the kind known in the United States."

The following story of the discovery of the largest two of these ruins, one of which is the subject of this article, is quoted from Nordenskiöld:[c]

The honour of the discovery of these remarkable ruins belongs to Richard and Alfred Wetherill of Mancos. The family own large herds of cattle, which

---

[a] Ancient Ruins in Southwestern Colorado, *in* Rep. U. S. Geol. and Geogr. Survey of the Ter., 1874, p. 369.

[b] Report on the Ancient Ruins of Southwestern Colorado, examined during the summers of 1875 and 1876, ibid., 1876, p. 383.

[c] The Cliff Dwellers of the Mesa Verde, pp. 12, 13, Stockholm, 1893.

wander about on the Mesa Verde. The care of these herds often calls for long rides on the mesa and in its labyrinth of cañons. During these long excursions ruins, the one more magnificent than the other, have been discovered. The two largest were found by Richard Wetherill and Charley Mason one December day in 1888, as they were riding together through the piñon wood on the mesa, in search of a stray herd. They had penetrated through the dense scrub to the edge of a deep cañon. In the opposite cliff, sheltered by a huge, massive vault of rock, there lay before their astonished eyes a whole town with towers and walls, rising out of a heap of ruins. This grand monument of bygone ages seemed to them well deserving of the name of the Cliff Palace. Not far from this place, but in a different cañon, they discovered on the same day another very large cliff-dwelling; to this they gave the name of Sprucetree House, from a great spruce that jutted forth from the ruins. During the course of years Richard and Alfred Wetherill have explored the mesa and its cañons in all directions; they have thus gained a more thorough knowledge of its ruins than anyone. Together with their brothers John, Clayton, and Wynn, they have also carried out excavations, during which a number of extremely interesting finds have been made. A considerable collection of these objects, comprising skulls, pottery, implements of stone, bone, and wood, etc., has been sold to "The Historical Society of Colorado." A still larger collection is in the possession of the Wetherill family. A brief catalogue of this collection forms the first printed notice of the remarkable finds made during the excavations.

Mr. F. H. Chapin visited the Mesa Verde ruins in 1889 and published illustrated accounts [a] of his visit containing much information largely derived from the Wetherills and others. Dr. W. R. Birdsall also published an account of these ruins,[b] illustrated by several figures. Neither Chapin nor Birdsall gives special attention to the ruin now called Spruce-tree House, and while their writings are interesting and valuable in the general history of the archeology of the Mesa Verde, they are of little aid in our studies of this particular ruin. The same may be said of the short and incomplete notices of the Mesa Verde ruins which have appeared in several newspapers. The scientific descriptions of Spruce-tree House as well as of other Mesa Verde ruins begin with the memoir of the talented Swede, Baron Gustav Nordenskiöld, who, in his work, The Cliff Dwellers of the Mesa Verde, gives the first comprehensive account of the ruins of this mesa. It is not too much to say that he has rendered to American archeology in this work a service which will be more and more appreciated in the future development of that science. In order to make more comprehensive the present author's report on Spruce-tree House, the following description of this ruin is quoted from Nordenskiöld's memoir (pp. 50–56):

A few hundred paces to the north along the cliff lead to a large cave, in the shadow of which lie the ruins of a whole village, *Sprucetree House.* This cave is 70 m. broad and 28 m. in depth. The height is small in comparison

---

[a] Cliff-dwellings of the Mancos Cañons, in *Appalachia,* vi, no. 1, Boston, May, 1890; *The American Antiquarian,* xii, 193, 1890; The Land of the Cliff Dwellers, 1892.

[b] The Cliff-dwellings of the Cañons of the Mesa Verde, in *Bulletin of the American Geographical Society,* xxiii, no. 4, 584, 1891.

with the depth, the interior of the cave thus being rather dark. The ground is fairly even and lies almost on a level, which has considerably facilitated the building operations. A plan of the ruins is given in Pl. IX. A great part of the house, or rather village, is in an excellent state of preservation, both the walls, which at some places are several stories high and rise to the roof of rock, and the floors between the different stories still remaining. The architecture is the same as that described in the ruins on Wetherill's Mesa. In some parts more care is perhaps displayed in the shape of the blocks and in the joints between them. The walls, here as in other cliff-dwellings, are about 0.3 m. thick, seldom more. A point which immediately strikes the eye in Pl. IX, is that no premeditated design has been followed in the erection of the buildings. It seems as if only a few rooms had first been built, additions having subsequently been made to meet the requirements of the increasing population. This circumstance, which I have already touched upon when describing other ruins, may be observed in most of the cliff-dwellings. There is further evidence to show that the whole village was not erected at the same time. At several places it may be seen that new walls have been added to the old, though the stones of both walls do not fit into each other, as is the case when two adjacent walls have been constructed simultaneously. The arrangement of the rooms has been determined by the surrounding cliff, the walls being generally built either at right angles or parallel to it. At some places the walls of several adjoining apartments of about equal size have been consistently erected in the same direction, some blocks of rooms thus possessing a regularity which is wanting in the cliff-village as a whole. This is perhaps the first stage in the development of the cliff-dwellings to the villages whose ruins are common in the valleys and on the mesa, and which are constructed according to a fixed design.

In the plan (Pl. IX) it may be seen that the cave contains two distinct groups of rooms. At about the middle of the cliff-village a kind of passage (23), uninterrupted by any wall, runs through the whole ruin. We found the remains, however, of a cross wall projecting from an elliptical room (14 in the plan) in the south part of the village. Each of these two divisions of the ruin contains an open space (16 and 28) at the back of the cave, the ground in both these places being covered with bird droppings. It is probable that this was the place where tame turkeys were kept, though it can not have been a very pleasant abode for them, for at least in the north of the ruin this part of the cave is almost pitch dark, the walls of the inner court (28), rising up to the roof of rock. In each of the two divisions of the cliff-village a number of estufas were built, in the north at least five, in the south at least two; while several more are, no doubt, buried in the heaps of ruins. These estufas preserve to the least detail the ordinary type (diam. 4–5 metres) fully described above. They are generally situated in front of the other rooms, with their foundations sunk deeper in the ground, and have never had an upper story. Even their site suggests that they were used for some special purpose, probably as assembly-rooms at religious festivities held by those members of the tribe who lived in the adjacent rooms. In all the estufas without exception the roof has fallen in. It is probable, as I have mentioned before, that the entrance of these rooms, as is still the case among the Pueblo Indians, was constructed in the roof. The other rooms were entered by narrow doorways (breadth 40–55 cm., height 65–80 cm.). These doorways are generally rectangular, often somewhat narrower at the top; the sill consists, as already described, of a long stone slab, the lintel of a few sticks a couple of centimetres in thickness, laid across the opening to support the wall above them. The arch was unknown to the builders of these villages, even in the form common among the ruins of Central America, and constructed by carrying the walls on both sides of the doorway nearer to each other as each course of stones was laid, until they could be joined by a stone slab placed across them. Along both sides of the doorway and under the lintel a narrow frame of thin sticks covered with plaster was built (see fig. 28 to the left). This frame, which leant inwards, served to support the door, a thin, flat, rectangular stone slab of suitable size. Through two loops on the outside of the wall, made of osiers inserted in the chinks between the stones, and placed one on each side of the doorway, a thin stick was passed, thus forming a kind of bolt. Besides this type of door most cliff-villages contain examples of another. Some doorways present the appearance shown in fig. 28 to the right (height 90 cm., breadth at the top, 45 cm., at the bottom 30 cm.) They were not closed with a stone slab. They probably belonged to the rooms most frequented in daily life, and were therefore fashioned so as to admit of more convenient ingress and egress. The other doorways, through which it is by no means easy to enter, probably belonged in general to storerooms or other chambers not so often visited and requiring for some reason or other a door to close them. It should be mentioned that the large, T-shaped doors described above are rare in the ruins on Wetherill's Mesa which both in architecture and in other respects bear traces of less care and skill on the part of the builders, and are also in a more advanced stage of decay, thus giving the impression of greater age than the ruins treated of in the present chapter, though without showing any essential differences.

The rooms, with the exception of the estufas, are nearly always rectangular, the sides measuring seldom more than two or three metres. North of the passage (23) which divides the ruin into two parts, a whole series of rooms (26, 29–33) still extends outwards from the back of the cave, their walls reaching up to the roof of rock, and the floors between the upper and lower stories being in a perfect state of preservation. The lower rooms are generally entered by small doors opening directly on the "street." In the interior the darkness is almost complete, especially in room 34, which has no direct communication with the passage. It must be approached either through 35, which is a narrow room with the short side towards the "street" entirely open, or through 33. We used 34 as a dark room for photographic purposes.

The walls and roof of some rooms are thick with soot. The inhabitants must have had no great pretensions as regards light and air. The doorways served also as windows, though at one or two places small, quadrangular loop-holes have been constructed in the walls for the passage of light. Entrance to the upper story is generally gained by a small quadrangular hole in the roof at a corner of the lower room, a foothold being afforded merely by some stones projecting from the walls. This hole was probably covered with a stone slab. like the doors. Thick beams of cedar or piñon and across them thin poles, laid close together, form the floors between the stories. In some cases long sticks were laid in pairs across the cedar beams at a distance of some decimeters between the pairs, a layer of twigs and cedar bast was placed over the sticks, and the whole was covered with clay, which was smoothed and dried.

In several other parts of the ruin besides this the walls still reach the roof of the cave. These walls are marked in the plan. In all the estufas and in some of the other rooms, perhaps the apartments of chiefs or families of rank, the walls are covered with a thin coat of yellow plaster. In one instance they are even decorated with a painting, representing two birds, which is reproduced in one of the following chapters. Pl. x: 2 shows a part of the ruin, situated in the north of the cave. The spot from which the photograph was taken, as well as the approximate angle of view, is marked in the plan. The left half of the photograph is occupied by a wall with doorways, rising to a height of three stories and up to the roof of the cave; within the wall lies a series of five rooms on the ground floor; behind these rooms the large open space mentioned above (28) occupies the depths of the cavern. Here the beams are all that remains of the floors of the upper stories, their ends projecting a foot or two beyond the wall between the second and third stories, where support was probably afforded in this manner to a balcony, as an easier means of communication between the rooms of the upper stories. In front of this part of the building, but not visible in the photograph, lie two estufas and outside the latter is a long wall. To judge by the ruins, the roofs of these estufas once lay on a level with the floors of the adjoining rooms, so that over the estufas, which were sunk in the ground, only the roofs being left visible, the inhabitants had an open space, bounded on the outside by the said long wall, which formed a rampart at the edge of the talus. The same method of construction is employed by the Moki Indians in their estufas; but these rooms are rectangular in form.—Farther north lies another estufa. Its site, nearest to the cliff wall, would seem to indicate that it is the oldest. The walls in the north of the ruin still rise to a height of 6 metres.

The south part of the ruin is similar in all respects to the north. Its only singularity is a room of elliptical shape (axes 3.6 and 2.9 m.); from this room a wall runs south, enclosing a small open space (16) where, as at the corresponding place in the north of the ruin, the ground is covered with bird droppings mixed with dust and refuse. At one end there are two semicircular enclosures (17, 18) of loose stones forming low walls. In a pentagonal room (8) south of this open space one corner contains a kind of closet (height 1.2 m., length and breadth 0.9 m.) composed of two large upright slabs of stone, with a third slab laid across them in a sloping position and cemented fast (see fig. 29). Of the use to which this "closet" was put, I am ignorant. Farther south some of the rooms are situated on a narrow ledge, along which a wall has been erected, probably for purposes of defense.

Plate x:1 is a photograph of Sprucetree House from the opposite side of the cañon. The illustrations give a better idea of the ruin's appearance than any description could do.

Our excavations in Sprucetree House lasted only a few days. This ruin will certainly prove a rich field for future researches.[a] Some handsome baskets and pieces of pottery were the best finds made during the short period of our excavations. In a room (69) belonging to the north part of the ruin we found the skeletons of three children who had been buried there.

A circumstance which deserves mention, and which was undoubtedly of great importance to the inhabitants of Sprucetree House, is the presence at the bottom of the cañon, a few hundred paces from the ruin, of a fairly good spring.

Near Sprucetree House there are a number of very small, isolated rooms, situated on ledges most difficult of access. One of these tiny cliff-dwellings may be seen to the left in fig. 27. It is improbable that these cells, which are sometimes so small that one can hardly turn in them, were really dwelling places; their object is unknown to me, unless it was one of defense, archers being posted there when danger threatened, so that the enemy might have to face a volley of arrows from several points at once. In such a position a few men could defend themselves, even against an enemy of superior force, for an assailant could reach the ledge only by climbing with hands and feet. Another explanation, perhaps better, was suggested to me by Mr. Fewkes. He thinks

---

[a] Since this was written, a well-preserved mummy has been found by Wetherill in the open space (28) at the very back of the cave. This is a further example of the burial of the dead in the open space between the village and the cliff wall behind it (see p. 47).— [NORDENSKIÖLD.]

that these small rooms were shrines where offerings to the gods were deposited. No object has, however, been found to confirm this suggestion.

To the right of fig. 27 a huge spruce may be seen. Its roots lie within the ruins of Sprucetree House, the trunk projecting from the wall of an estufa. In Pl. x:1 the tree is wanting. I had it cut down in order to ascertain its age. We counted the rings, which were very distinct, twice over, the results being respectively 167 and 169. I had supposed from the thickness of the tree that the number of the rings was much greater.

GENERAL FEATURES

Like the majority of cliff-dwellings in the Mesa Verde National Park, Spruce-tree House stands in a recess protected above by an overhanging cliff. Its form is crescentic, following that of the cave and extending approximately north and south.

The author has given the number of rooms and their dimensions in his report to the Secretary of the Interior (published in the latter's report for 1907–8) from which he makes the following quotation:

The total length of Spruce-tree House was found to be 216 feet, its width at the widest part 89 feet. There were counted in the Spruce-tree House 114 rooms, the majority of which were secular, and 8 ceremonial chambers or kivas. Nordenskiöld numbered 80 of the former and 7 of the latter, but in this count he apparently did not differentiate in the former those of the first, second and third stories. Spruce-tree House was in places 3 stories high; the third-story rooms had no artificial roof, but the wall of the cave served that purpose. Several rooms, the walls of which are now two stories high, formerly had a third story above the second, but their walls have now fallen, leaving as the only indication of their former union with the cave lines destitute of smoke on the top of the cavern. Of the 114 rooms, at least 14 were uninhabited, being used as storage and mortuary chambers. If we eliminate these from the total number of rooms we have 100 enclosures which might have been dwellings. Allowing 4 inhabitants for each of these 100 rooms would give about 400 persons as an aboriginal population of Spruce-tree House. But it is probable that this estimate should be reduced, as not all the 100 rooms were inhabited at the same time, there being evidence that several of them had occupants long after others were deserted. Approximately, Spruce-tree House had a population not far from 350 people, or about 100 more than that of Walpi, one of the best-known Hopi pueblos.[a]

In the rear of the houses are two large recesses used for refuse-heaps or for burial of the dead. From the abundance of guano and turkey bones it is supposed that turkeys were kept in these places for ceremonial or other purposes. Here have been found several desiccated human bodies commonly called mummies.

The ruin is divided by a street into two sections, the northern and the southern, the former being the more extensive. Light is prevented from entering the larger of these recesses by rooms which reach the roof of the cave. In front of these rooms are circular sub-

[a] On the author's plan of Spruce-tree House from a survey by Mr. S. G. Morley, the third story is indicated by crosshatching, the second by parallel lines, while the first has no markings. (Pl. 1.)

terranean rooms called *kivas*, which are sunken below the surrounding level places, or plazas, the roofs of these kivas having been formerly level with the plazas.

The front boundary of these plazas is a wall [a] which when the excavations were begun was buried under débris of fallen walls, but which formerly stood several feet above the level of the plazas.

MAJOR ANTIQUITIES

Under this term are included those immovable prehistoric remains which, taken together, constitute a cliff-dwelling. The architectural features—walls of rooms and structures connected with them, as beams, balconies, fireplaces—are embraced in the term "major antiquities." None of these can be removed from their sites without harm, so they must be protected in the place where they now stand.

In a valuable article on the ruins in valley of the San Juan and its tributaries, Dr. T. Mitchell Prudden [b] recognizes in this region what he designates a "unit type;" that is, a ruin consisting of a kiva backed by a row of rooms generally situated on its north side, with lateral extensions east and west, and a burial place on the opposite, or south, side of the kiva. This form of "unit type," as he points out, is more apparent in ruins situated in an open country than in those built in cliffs. The same form may be recognized in Spruce-tree House, which is composed of several "unit types" arranged side by side. The simplicity of these "unit types" is somewhat modified, however, in this as in all cliff-dwellings, by the form of the site. The author would amend Prudden's definition of the "unit type" as applied to cliff-houses by adding to the latter's description a bounding wall connecting the two lateral extensions of the row of rooms, thus forming the south side of the enclosure of the kiva. For obvious reasons, in this amended description the burial place is absent, as it does not occur in the position assigned to it in the original description.

PLAZAS AND COURTS

As before stated, the buildings of Spruce-tree House are divided into a northern and a southern section by a street which penetrates from plaza G to the rear of the cave. (Pl. 1.) The northern section is not only the larger, but there is evidence that it is also the older. It is bounded by some of the best-constructed buildings, situated along the north side of the street. The rooms of the southern section are less numerous, although in some respects more instructive.

[b] See *American Anthropologist*, n. s., v. no. 2, 224–288, 1903.
[a] See H. R. No. 3703, 58th Cong., 3d sess., 1905—The Ruined Cliff Dwellings in Ruin and Navajo Canyons, in the Mesa Verde, Colorado, by Coert Dubois.

There are practically the same number of plazas as of kivas in this ruin. With the exception of C and D, each plaza is occupied by a single kiva, the roof of which constitutes the central part of the floor of the square enclosure (plaza). The plazas commonly contain remnants of small shrines, fireplaces, and corn-grinding bins, and are perforated by mysterious holes evidently used in ceremonies. Their floors are hardened by the tramping of the many feet that passed over them. The best preserved of all the plazas is that which contains kiva G. It can hardly be supposed that the roof of kiva A served as a dance place, which is the ordinary office of a plaza, but it may have been used in ceremonies. The largest plaza of the series, in the rear of which are rooms while the front is inclosed by the bounding wall, is that containing kivas C and D. The appearance of this plaza before and after clearing out and repairing is shown in plate 3; the view was taken from the north end of the ruin.

From the number of fireplaces and similar evidences it may be concluded that the street already mentioned as dividing the village into two sections served many purposes. Most important of these was its use as the open-air dwellings of the villagers. Its hardened clay floor suggests the constant passage of many feet. Its surface slopes gradually downward from the back of the cave, ending at a step near the round room in the rear of kiva G. This step marks also the eastern boundary of the plaza (G) which contains the best-preserved of all the ceremonial rooms of Spruce-tree House.

The discovery by excavation of the wall that originally formed the front of the village was important. In this way was revealed a correct ground plan of the ruin (pl. 1) which had never before been traced by archeologists. When the work began, this wall was deeply buried under accumulated débris, its course not being visible to any considerable extent. By removing the fallen stones composing the débris the wall could be readily traced. In the repair work the original stones were replaced in the structure. As in the first instance this wall was probably about as high as the head, it may have been used for protection. The only openings are small rectangular orifices, the presence of one opposite the external opening of the air flue of each kiva suggesting that formerly these flues opened outside the wall. Two kivas, B and F, are situated west of this wall and therefore outside the village. There are evidences of a walk on top of the talus along the front of the pueblo outside the front wall, and of a retaining wall to prevent the edge of the talus from wearing away. (Pls. 4, 5.)

CONSTRUCTION OF WALLS

The walls of Spruce-tree House were built of stones generally laid in mortar but sometimes piled on one another, the joints being pointed later. Sections of walls in which no mortar was used occur on the tops of other walls.   These dry walls served among other purposes to shield the roofs of adjacent buildings from snow and rain.   Whenever mortar was used it appears that a larger quantity was employed than was necessary, the effect being to weaken the wall since the pointing washed out quickly, being less capable than stone of resisting erosion.   When the mortar wore away, the wall was left in danger of falling of its own weight.   The pointing was generally done with the hands, the superficial impressions of which show in several places. Small flakes of stone or fragments of pottery were sometimes inserted in the joints, serving both as a decoration, and as a protection by preventing the rapid wearing away of the mortar.   Little pellets of clay were also used in the joints for the same purpose.

The character of masonry in different rooms varies considerably, in some places showing good, in others poor, workmanship.   As a rule the construction of the corners is weak, the stones forming them being rarely bonded or tied.   Component stones of the walls seldom break joints; thus a well-known device by means of which walls are strengthened is lacking, and consequently cracks are numerous and the work is unstable.   Fully half the stones used in construction were hammered or dressed into desirable shapes, the remainder being laid as they were gathered, with their flat surfaces exposed when possible. (Pls. 6, 7.)

Some of the walls were out of plumb when constructed and the faces of many were never straight.   The walls show evidences of having been repeatedly repaired, as indicated by a difference in color of the mortar used.

Plasters of different colors, as red, white, yellow, and brown, were used.   The lower half of the wall of a room was generally painted brownish red, the upper half often white.   There are evidences of several coats of plastering, especially on the walls of the kivas, some of which are much discolored with smoke.

The replastering of the walls of Hopi kivas is an incident of the *Powamû* festival, or ceremonial purification of the fields commonly called the "Bean planting," which occurs every February.   On a certain day of this festival girls thoroughly replaster the four walls of the kivas and at the close of the work leave impressions of their hands in white mud on the kiva beams.

The rooms of Spruce-tree House may be considered under two headings: secular rooms, and ceremonial rooms, or kivas. The former are rectangular, the latter circular, in form.

SECULAR ROOMS

The secular rooms are the more numerous in Spruce-tree House. In order to designate them in future descriptions they were numbered from 1 to 71, in black paint, in conspicuous places on the walls.

(Pl. 1.) This enumeration begins at the north end and passes thence to the south end of the ruin, but in one or two instances this order is not followed. The author has given below a brief reference to some of the important secular rooms in the series.

The foundations of room 1 were apparently built on a fallen bowlder, the entrance being reached by means of a series of stone steps built into the side hill. The floor of this room is on the level of the second story of other rooms, being continuous with the top of kiva A. It is probable that when this kiva was constructed it was found impossible to make it subterranean on account of the solid rock. A retaining wall was built outside the kiva and the intervening space was filled with earth in order to impart to the room a subterranean character.

Room 2 has three stories, or tiers, of rooms. The floor of the second story, which is the roof of the first, is well preserved, the sides of the hatchway, or means of passage from one room to the one below it, being almost entire. This room possesses a feature which is unique. The base of its south wall is supported by curved timbers, whose ends rest on walls, while the middle is supported by a pillar of masonry. (Pl. 8.) The T-shaped door in this wall faces south. It is difficult to understand how the aperture could have been of any use as a doorway unless there was a balcony below it. and no sign of such structure is now visible. The west wall of rooms 2 and 3 was built on top of a fallen rock from which it rises precipitously to a considerable height. The floor of room 4, which lies in front of kiva A, is on a level with the roof of the kiva, and somewhat higher than the surface of the neighboring plaza but not higher than the roof of the first story. As the floors of room 1 and room 4 are on the same level, it would appear that both were considerably elevated or so constructed otherwise that the kiva should be subterranean. This endeavor to render the kiva subterranean by building up around it, when conditions made it impossible to excavate in the solid rock, is paralleled in some other Mesa Verde ruins.

The ventilator of kiva A, as will be seen later, does not open through the front wall, as is usually the case, but on one side. This is accounted for by the presence of a room on this side of the kiva. Rooms 2, 3, 4 were constructed after the walls of kiva A were built, hence several modifications were necessary in the prescribed plan of building these rooms.

The foundation of the inclosure, 5, conforms on one side to the outer wall of the village, and on the other to the curvature of kiva B. As this inclosure does not seem ever to have been roofed, it is probable that it was not a house. A fireplace at one end indicates that cooking was formerly done here. It is instructive to note that the front wall of the ruin begins at this place.

Rooms 6, 7, 8, which lie side by side, closely resemble one another, having much in common. They were evidently dwellings, and may have been sleeping-places for families. Rooms 7 and 8 were two stories high, the floor of no. 8 being on a level with the adjoining plaza. Room 9 is so unusual in its construction that it can not be regarded as a living room. It was used as a mortuary chamber, evidences being strong that it was opened from time to time for new interments. Room 12 also was a ceremonial chamber, and, like the preceding, will be considered later at greater length. The walls of the two rooms, 10 and 11, are low, projecting into plaza C, of whose border they form a part. Near them, or in one corner of the same plaza, is a bin, the sides of which are formed of stone slabs set on edge. The use of this bin is problematical.

The front wall of room 15 had been almost wholly destroyed before the repair work began, and was so unstable that it was necessary to erect a buttress to support it. This room, which is one story high, is irregular in shape; its doorways open into rooms 14 and 16. The walls of rooms 16 and 18 extend to the roof of the cave, shutting out the light on one side from the great refuse-place in the rear of the cliff-dwellings. The openings through the walls of these rooms into this darkened area have been much broken by vandals, and the walls greatly damaged. Room 17, like 16 and 18, is somewhat larger than most of the apartments in Spruce-tree House.

Theoretically it may be supposed that when Spruce-tree House was first settled it had one clan occupying a cluster of rooms, 1–11, and one ceremonial room, kiva A. As the place grew three other "unit types" centering about kivas C–H were added, and still later each of these units was enlarged and new kivas were built in each section. Thus A was enlarged by addition of B; C by addition of D; E by addition of F; and G was subordinated to H. In this way the rooms near the kivas grew in numbers. The block of rooms designated 50–53 is not accounted for, however, in this theory.

Rooms numbered 19–22 are instructive. Their walls are well preserved and form the east side of plaza C. These walls extend from the level of the plaza to the top of the cavern, and in places show some of the best masonry in Spruce-tree House. Just in front of room 19, situated on the left-hand side as one enters the doorway, is a covered recess, where probably ceremonial bread was baked or otherwise cooked. This place bears a strong resemblance to recesses found in Hopi villages, especially as in its floor is set a cooking-pot made of earthenware. Rooms 19–21 are two stories high; there are fireplaces in the corners and doorways on the front sides. The upper stories were approached and entered by balconies. The holes in which formerly rested the beams that supported these balconies can be clearly seen.

Rooms 21 and 22 are three stories high, the entrances to the three tiers being seen in the accompanying view (pl. 6). The beams that once supported the balcony of the third story resemble those of the first story; they project from the wall that forms the front of room 29.

The external entrance to room 24 opens directly on the plaza. Some of the rafters of this room still remain, and near the rear door is a projecting wall, in the corner of which is a fireplace. Although room 25 is three stories high, it does not reach to the cave top. None of the roofs of the rooms one over another are intact, and the west side of the second and third stories is very much broken. The plaster of the second-story walls is decorated with mural paintings that will be considered more fully under Pictographs. It is not evident how entrance through the doorway of the second story was made unless we suppose that there was a notched log, or ladder, for that purpose resting on the ground. In order to strengthen the north wall of room 25 it was braced against the walls of outer rooms by constructing masonry above the doorway that leads from plaza D to room 26. This tied all three walls together and imparted corresponding strength to the whole.

The lower-story walls of room 26 are in fairly good condition, having needed but little repair. There is a good fireplace in the floor at the northeast corner. Excavations revealed a passageway from kiva D into room 26, the opening into the upper room being situated near its north wall. The west wall of room 26 is curved. The walls of rooms 27 and 28 are much dilapidated, the portion of the western section that remains being continuous with the front wall of the pueblo. A small mural fragment ending blindly arises from the outside of the west wall of room 27. This is believed to have been part of a small enclosure used for cooking purposes. Much repairing was necessary in the walls of rooms 27 and 28, since they were situated almost directly in the way of torrents of water which in time of rains fall over the rim of the canyon.

The block of rooms numbered 30–44, situated east of kiva E, have the most substantial masonry and are the best constructed of any in Spruce-tree House. (Pl. 9.) As room 45 is only a dark passageway it should be considered more a street than a dwelling. Rooms 30–36 are one story each in height, rectangular in shape, roofless, and of about the same dimensions; of these room 35 is perhaps the best preserved, having well-constructed fireplaces in one corner. Rooms 37, 38, 39 are built deep in the cavern; their walls, especially those of 38, are very much broken down. There would seem to be hardly a possibility that these rooms were inhabited, especially after the construction of the rooms in front of the cave which shut off all light. But they may easily have served as storage places. Their walls were constructed of well-dressed stones and afford an example of good masonry work.

Here and there are indications of other rooms in the darker parts of the cave. In some instances their walls extended to the roof of the cave where their former position is indicated by light bands on the sooty surface.

Rooms 40–47 are among the finest chambers in Spruce-tree House. Rooms 48 and 49 are very much damaged, the walls having fallen, leaving only the foundations above the ground level. Several rooms in this part of the ruin, especially rooms 43 (pl. 9) and 44, still have roofs and floors as well preserved as when they were built, and although dark, owing to lack of windows, they have fireplaces in the corners, the smoke escaping apparently through the diminutive door openings. The thresholds of some of the doorways are too high above the main court to be entered without ladders or notched poles, but projecting stones or depressions for the feet, still visible, apparently assisted the inhabitants, as they do modern visitors, to enter rooms 41 and 42.

Each of the small block of rooms 50–53 is one story and without a roof, but possessing well-preserved ground floors. In room 53 there is a depression in the floor at the bottom of which is a small hole.[a]

In the preceding pages there have been considered the rooms of the north section of Spruce-tree House, embracing dwellings, ceremonial rooms, and other enclosures north of the main court, and the space in the rear called the refuse-heap—in all, six circular ceremonial rooms and a large majority of the living and storage rooms. From all the available facts at the author's disposal it is supposed that this portion is older than the south section, which contains but two ceremonial rooms and not more than a third the number of secular dwellings.[b]

The cluster of rooms connected with kivas G and H shows signs of having been built by a clan which may have joined Spruce-tree House subsequent to the construction of the north section of the village. The ceremonial rooms in this section differ in form from the others. Here occur two round rooms or towers, duplicates of which have not been found in the north section.

Room 61 in the south section of Spruce-tree House has a closet made of flat stones set on edge and covered with a perforated stone slab slightly inclined from the horizontal.

The inclosures at the extreme south end, which follow a narrow ledge, appear to have been unroofed passages rather than rooms. On

---

[a] In Hopi dwellings the author has often seen a provisional *sipapû* used in household ceremonies.

[b] The proportion of kivas to dwellings in any village is not always the same in prehistoric pueblos, nor is there a fixed ratio in modern pueblos. It would appear that there is some relation between the number of kivas and the number of inhabitants, but what that relation is, numerically, has never been discovered.

ledges somewhat higher there are small granaries each with a hole in the side,. probably for the storage of corn.

It will be noticed that the terraced form of buildings, almost universal in modern three-story pueblos and common in pictures of ruins south of the San Juan, does not exist in Spruce-tree House. The front of the three tiers of rooms 22, 23, as shown in plate 3, is vertical, not terraced from foundation to top. Whether the walls of rooms now in ruins were terraced or not can not be determined, for these have been washed out and have fallen to so great an extent that it is almost impossible to tell their original form. Rooms 25–28, for instance, might have been terraced on the front side, but it is more reasonable to suppose they were not;[a] from the arrangement of doors it would seem that there was a lateral entrance on the ground floor rather than through roofs.

BALCONIES

Balconies attached to the walls of buildings below rows of doors occurred at several places. On no other hypothesis than the presence of these structures can be explained the elevated situation of entrances opening into the rooms immediately above rooms 20, 21, 22. In fact, there appear to have been two balconies at this place, one above the other, but all now left of them is the projecting floor-beams, and a fragment of a floor on the projections at the north end of the lower one, in front of room 20. These balconies (pl. 3) were apparently constructed in the same way as the structure that gives the name to the ruin called Balcony House; they seem to have been used by the inhabitants as a means of communication between neighboring rooms.

Nordenskiöld writes:[b]

The second story is furnished along the wall just mentioned, with a balcony; the joists between the two stories project a couple of feet, long poles lie across them parallel to the walls, the poles are covered with a layer of cedar bast, and, finally with dried clay.

---

[a] Nordenskiöld on the contrary seems to make the terraced rooms one of the points of resemblance between the cliff-dwellings and the great ruins of the Chaco. He writes:

"On comparison of the ruins in Chaco Cañon with the cliff-dwellings of Mancos, we find several points of resemblance. In both localities the villages are fortified against attack, in the tract of Mancos by their site in inaccessible precipices, in Chaco Cañon by a high outer wall in which no doorways were constructed to afford entrance to an enemy. Behind this outer wall the rooms descended in terraces towards the inner court. One side of this court was protected by a lower semicircular wall. In the details of the buildings we can find several features common to both. The roofs between the stories were constructed in the same way. The doorways were built of about the same dimensions. The rafters were often allowed to project beyond the outer wall as a foundation for a sort of balcony (Balcony House, the Pueblo Chettro Kettle). The estufa at Hungo Pavie with its six quadrangular pillars of stone is exactly similar to a Mesa Verde estufa (see p. 16). The pottery strewn in fragments everywhere in Chaco Cañon resembles that found on the Mesa Verde. We are thus not without grounds for assuming that it was the same people, at different stages of its development, that inhabitated these two regions."—The Cliff Dwellers of the Mesa Verde, p. 127.

[b] Ibid., p. 67.

FIREPLACES

There are many fireplaces in Spruce-tree House, in rooms, plazas, and courts. From their number it is evident that most of the cooking must have been done by the ancients in the courts and plazas, rather than in the houses. The rooms are so small and so poorly ventilated that it would not be possible for any one to remain in them when fires are burning.

The top of the cave in which Spruce-tree House is built is covered with soot, showing that formerly there were many fires in the courts and other open places of the village. In almost every corner of the buildings in which a fire could be made the effect of smoke on the adjoining walls is discernible, while ashes are found in a depression in the floor. These fireplaces are very simple, consisting simply of square box-like structures bounded by a few flat stones set on edge. In other instances a depression in the floor bordered with a low ridge of adobe served as a fireplace. There remains nothing to indicate that the inhabitants were familiar with chimneys or firehoods as is the case among the modern pueblos. Certain small rooms suggest cook-houses, or places where *piki*, or paper bread, was fried by the women on slabs of stone over a fire, but none of these slabs were found in place. The fireplaces of the kivas are considered specially in an account of the structure of those rooms (see p. 18).

No evidence that Spruce-tree House people burnt coal was observed, although they were familiar with lignite and seams of coal underlie their messa.

DOORS AND WINDOWS

There are both doors and windows in the secular houses of Spruce-tree House, although the two rarely exist together. The windows, most of which are small square peep-holes or round orifices, look obliquely downward, as if their purpose was rather for outlook than for air, the latter being admitted as a rule through the doorway. (Pls. 10, 11.)

The two types of doorways differ more in shape than in any other feature. These types may be called the rectangular and the T-shaped form. Both are found at a high level, but it can not be discovered how they could have been entered without ladders or notched logs. Although these modes of entrance were apparently often used it is remarkable that no traces of the logs have yet been found in the extensive excavations at Spruce-tree House. The T-shaped doorways are often filled in at the lower or narrow part, sometimes with stones rudely placed, oftentimes with good masonry, by which a T-shaped door is converted into one of square type. Doorways of both types are often completely filled in, leaving only their outlines on the sides of the wall.

FLOORS AND ROOFS

The floors of the rooms are all smoothly plastered and, although purposely broken through in places by those in search of specimens, are otherwise in fairly good condition. In one of the rooms at the left of the main court is a small round hole at the bottom of a concave depression like a fireplace, the use of which is not known. Many of the floors sound hollow when struck, but this fact is not an indication of the presence of cavities below. In tiers of rooms that rise above the first story the roof of one room forms the floor of the room above it. Wherever roofs still remain they are found to be well-constructed (pl. 9) and to resemble those of the old Hopi houses. In Spruce-tree House the roofs are supported by timbers laid from one wall to another; these in turn support crossbeams on which were placed layers of cedar bark covered with a thick coating of mud. In several roofs hatchways are still to be seen, but in most cases entrances are at the sides. One second-story room has a fireplace constructed like those on the ground floor or on the roof. Several fireplaces were found on the roofs of buildings one story high.

The largest slabs of stone used in the construction of the rooms of Spruce-tree House were generally made into lintels and thresholds. The latter surfaces were often worn smooth by those crawling through the opening and in some cases they show grooves for the insertion of the door slabs. Although the sides of the door are often upright slabs of stone these may be replaced by boards set in adobe plaster. Similar split boards often form lintels.

The door was apparently a flat stone set in an adobe casing on the inside of the frame where it was held in position by a stick. Each end of this stick was inserted into an eyelet made of bent osiers firmly set in the wall. Many of these broken eyelets can still be seen in the doorways and one or two are still entire. A slab of stone closing one of the doorways is still in place.

KIVAS

There are eight circular subterranean rooms identified as ceremonial rooms, or *kivas*, in Spruce-tree House (pls. 12, 13). Beginning on the north these kivas are designated by letters A–H. When excavation began small depressions full of fallen stones, with here and there a stone buttress projecting out of the débris, were the only indications of the sites of these important chambers. The walls of kiva H were the most dilapidated and the most obscured of all, the central portion of the front wall of rooms 62 and 63 having fallen into this chamber; added to the débris were the high walls of the round room, no. 69. Kiva G is the best-preserved kiva and kiva A the most exceptional in construction. Kiva B, never seen by previous investigators, was in poor condition, its walls being almost completely broken down.   Part of the wall of kiva A is double (pl. 13), indicating a circular room built inside another room the shape of which inclines to oval, the former utilizing a portion of the wall of the latter.   This kiva is also exceptional in being surrounded on three sides by rooms, the fourth side being the wall of the cavern.   From several considerations the author regards this as the oldest kiva in Spruce-tree House.

The typical structure of a Spruce-tree House kiva is as follows: Its form is circular or oval; the site is subterranean, the roof being level with the floor of the surrounding plaza.   (Pls. 13–15.)   Two walls, an outer and an inner, inclose the room, the latter forming the lower part.   Upon the top of this lower wall rest six pedestals, which support the roof beams; the outer wall braces these pedestals on one side. The spaces between these pedestals form recesses in which the floors extend a few feet above the floor of the room.

The floor of the kiva is generally plastered, but in some cases is solid rock.   The fireplace is a circular depression in the floor, its purpose being indicated by the wood ashes found therein.   Its lining is ordinarily made of clay, which in some instances is replaced by stones set on edge.

The other important opening in the floor is one called sipapû, or symbolic opening into the underworld.   This is generally situated near the center of the room, opposite the fireplace.   This opening into the underworld is barely large enough to admit the human hand and extends only about a foot below the floor surface.   It is commonly single, but in one kiva two of these orifices were detected.   A similar symbolic opening occurs in modern Hopi kivas, as has been repeatedly described in the author's accounts of pueblo ceremonials.   An important structure of a Spruce-tree House kiva is an upright slab of rock, or a narrow thin wall of masonry, placed between the fireplace and the wall of the kiva.   This object, sometimes called an altar, serves as a deflector, its function being to distribute the air which enters the kiva at the floor level through a vertical shaft, or ventilator.   Every kiva has at least one such deflector, a single fireplace, and the sipapû, or ceremonial opening mentioned above.

Several small cubby-holes, or receptacles for paint or small ceremonial objects, generally occur in the lower walls of the kiva.   In addition to these there exist openings ample in size to admit the human body, which serve different purposes.   The first kind communicate directly with passageways through which one can pass from the kiva into a neighboring room or plaza.   Such a passageway in kiva E has steps near the opening in the floor of room 35.   This entrance is not believed, however, to be the only way by which one could enter or leave this room. but was a private passage, the main entrance being through the roof. Another lateral passageway is found in kiva D, where there is an opening in the south wall communicating with the open air by means of an exit in the floor of room 26; another opening is found in the wall on the east side. Kiva C has a lateral opening communicating with a vertical passageway which opens in the middle of the neighboring plaza. In addition to lateral openings all kivas without exception have others that serve as ventilators, as before mentioned, by which air is introduced on the floor level of the kivas. The opening of this kind communicates through a horizontal passage with a vertical flue which finds its way outside the room on a level with the roof. In cases where the kiva is situated near the front wall these ventilators open through this wall by means of square apertures. All ventilator openings are in the west wall except that of kiva A, which is the only one that has rooms on that side.

The construction of kiva roofs must have been a difficult problem (pls. 14, 15). The beams (L–1 to L–4) are supported by the six pedestals (C) which stand upon the banquettes (A), and in turn are supported by the outer wall (B) of the kiva. On top of each of these pedestals is inserted a short stick (H) that served as a peg on which the inmates hung their ceremonial paraphernalia. The supports of the roof were cedar logs cut in suitable lengths by stone axes· Three logs were laid, connecting adjacent pedestals upon which they rested. These logs, which were large enough to support considerable weight, had been stripped of their bark. Upon these six beams were laid an equal number of beams, spanning the intervals between those first placed, as shown in the illustration (pl. 15). Upon the last-mentioned beams were still other logs extending across the kiva, as also shown in the plate.

The main weight of the roof was supported by two large logs which extended diametrically across the kiva from one wall to the wall opposite; they were placed a short distance apart, parallel with each other. The distance between these logs determines the width of the doorway, two sides of which they form. The other two sides are formed by two beams (L–4) of moderate size, laid across these logs, the space between them and the two beams being filled in with other logs, forming a compact framework. No nails are necessary in a roof constructed in this way.

The smaller interstices between the logs were filled in with small sticks and twigs, thus preventing soil from dropping into the room. Over the supports of the roof was spread a layer of cedar bark (M) covered with mud (N), laid deep enough to bring the top of the roof to the level of the plaza in which the kiva is situated.

No kiva was found in which the plastering of the walls was supported by sticks, as sometimes occurs here, according to Nordenskiöld, and in one or more of the Hopi kivas. The plastering of the walls was placed directly on the masonry.

It is probable that the kiva walls were painted with various devices before their roofs fell in and other mutilation of the walls took place. Among these designs parallel lines in white were common. Similar lines are still made with meal on kiva walls in Hopi ceremonies, as the author has often described. One of the pedestals of kiva A is decorated with a triangular figure on the margin of the dado, to which reference will be made later.

The author has found no conclusive answer to the question why the kivas are built under ground and are circular in form. He believes both conditions to be survivals of ancient " pit-houses," or subterranean dwellings of an antecedent people. In this explanation the kiva is regarded as the oldest form of building in the cliff-dwellings. We have the authority of observation bearing on this point. Pit-dwellings are recorded from several ruins. In a recent work Dr. Walter Hough figures and describes certain dwellings of subterranean character that are sometimes found in clusters,[a] while the present author has observed subterranean rooms so situated as to leave no doubt of their great antiquity.[b]

The form of the kiva is characteristic and may be used as a basis of classification of pueblo culture. The people whose kivas are circular inhabited villages now ruins in the valley of the San Juan and its tributaries, in Chelly canyon, Chaco canyon, and on the western plateau of the Rio Grande.

The rectangular kiva is a structure altogether different from a round kiva, morphologically, genetically, and geographically. It is peculiar to the southern and western pueblo area, and while of later growth, should not be regarded as an evolution from the circular kiva. Several authors have found in circular kivas survivals of nomadic architectural conditions, while the position of these rooms, in nearly every instance in front of the other rooms of the cliff-dwelling, has led others to accept the theory that they were later additions to the village, which should be ascribed to a different race. It would seem that this hypothesis hardly conforms to facts, as some kivas have secular rooms in front of them which show evidences of later construction. The strongest objection to the theory that kivas are modified houses of nomads is the style of roof construction.

KIVA A

This room (pl. 13), which is the most northerly of all of the ceremonial rooms of Spruce-tree House, is, the author believes, the

---

[a] *Bulletin 35 of the Bureau of American Ethnology,* Antiquities of the Upper Gila and Salt River Valleys in Arizona and New Mexico.

[b] In some cases the walls of the later rectangular rooms are built across and above them, as in compound B in the Casa Grande group of ruins.

oldest. In construction this is a remarkable chamber. It is built directly under the cliff, which forms part of its walls. In addition to its site the remarkable features are its double walls, and its floor on the level of the roofs of the other kivas. Although this kiva is not naturally subterranean, the earth and walls built up around it make it to all intents below the surface of the ground.

It appears from the arrangement of walls and banquettes that there is here presented an example of one room constructed inside of another, the inner room utilizing for its wall a portion of the outer. The inner room is more nearly circular than the outer in which it was subsequently built. In this inner room as in other kivas there are six banquettes, and the same number of pedestals to support the roof. Three of these pedestals are common to both rooms. The floor of this room shows nothing peculiar. It has a fire hole, a sipapû, and a deflector, or low wall between the fire hole and the entrance into the horizontal passageway of the ventilator. The ventilator itself opens just outside the west wall through a passageway, the walls of which stand on the wall of a neighboring room. No plaza of any considerable size surrounded the top of this kiva.

In order to get an idea as to how many rectangular rooms naturally accompany a single kiva, the author examined the ground plans of such cliff-dwellings as are known to have but one circular kiva, the majority of these being in the Chelly canyon. While it was not possible to determine the point satisfactorily, it was found that in several instances the circular kiva lies in the middle of several rooms, a fact which would seem to indicate that it was built first and that the square rooms were added later. Several clusters of rooms, each cluster having one kiva, closely resemble kiva A and its surroundings, in both form and structure.

KIVA B

The walls of this subterranean room had escaped all previous observers. They are very much dilapidated, being wholly concealed when work of excavation began. A large old cedar tree growing in the middle of this room led the author to abandon its complete excavation, which promised little return either in enlarging our knowledge of the ground plan of Spruce-tree House or in shedding additional light on the culture of its prehistoric inhabitants.

KIVAS C AND D

The two kivas, C and D, the roofs of which form the greater part of plaza C, logically belong together in our consideration. One of these rooms, C, was roofed over by the author, who followed as a model the roofs of the two kivas of the House with the Square Tower (Peabody House); the other shows a few log supports of an original roof—the only Spruce-tree House kiva of which this is true.

Not only was the roof of the kiva restored but its walls were well repaired, so that it now presents all the essential features of an ancient kiva. On one of the banquettes of this room the author found a vase which was evidently a receptacle for pigments or other ceremonial paraphernalia.

Kiva D has a passageway leading into room 26 and a second opening in the west wall on the floor level, besides a ventilator of the type common to all kivas. The top of the opening in the west wall appears covered with a flat stone in one of the photographic views (plate 11).

The wall in front of the village in the neighborhood of kivas C and D was wholly concealed by débris when work was begun on this part of the ruin. Excavation of this débris showed that opposite each kiva there was an opening with which the ventilator is believed formerly to have been connected. There seems to have been a low-storied house, possibly a cooking-place, provided with a roof, in an interval between kivas C and D; in the floor of the plaza at this point a well-made fire hole was uncovered.

KIVA E

Kiva E is one of the finest which was excavated, showing all the typical structures of these characteristic rooms; it almost fills the plaza in which it is situated. The exceptional feature of this room is a passageway through the west wall. Room 35 may have been the house of a chief or of a priest who kept in it his masks or other ceremonial paraphernalia. A similar opening in the wall of one of the Hopi kivas communicates with a dark room in which are kept altars and other ceremonial objects. When such a passageway into a dark chamber is not in use it is closed by a slab of stone.

KIVA F

Kiva F might be designated the Spruce-tree kiva from the large spruce tree that formerly grew near its outer wall. Its stump is now visible, but the tree lies extended in the canyon.

The walls of this kiva were poorly preserved, and only two of the pedestals were in place. The walls were repaired and the roof restored. This room is situated outside the walls, and in that respect recalls kiva B, described above. The ventilator opening of this kiva is situated on the south instead of on the west side of the room, as is the rule in other kivas. The large size of this room would indicate that it was of great importance in the religious ceremonials of the prehistoric inhabitants of Spruce-tree House, but all indications point to its late construction.[a]

---

[a] An examination of the best of previous maps of Spruce-tree House shows only a dotted line to indicate the location of this kiva.

KIVA G

Kiva G was so well preserved that its walls were thoroughly restored; it now stands as typical of one of these rooms in which the several characteristic features may be seen. For the guidance of visitors, letters or numbers accompanied by explanatory labels were painted by the author on the walls of the kiva.

Kiva G lies just below and in front of the round tower of Spruce-tree House, which is situated in the neighborhood of the main court, and may therefore be looked on as one of the most important kivas in the cliff-dwelling.[a] The solid stone floor of this room had been cut down about 8 inches.

KIVA H

Kiva H, the largest in Spruce-tree House, contained some of the best specimens excavated by the author. Its shape is oval rather than circular, and it fills the whole space inclosed by walls of rooms on three sides. In the neighborhood of kiva H is a comparatively spacious plaza which is bounded on the front by a low wall, now repaired, and on the other sides are high rooms. The plaza containing this kiva was ample for ceremonial dances which undoubtedly formerly occurred in it. The walls of kiva H formerly had a marked pinkish color, showing no sign of blackening by smoke except in places. Charred roof beams were excavated at one place, however, and charcoal occurred deep under the débris that filled this room.

CIRCULAR ROOMS OTHER THAN KIVAS

There are two rooms (nos. 54, 69) of circular shape in Spruce-tree House, one of which resembles the " tower " in the Cliff Palace. This room (no. 54) is situated to the right hand of the main court above referred to, into which it projects without attachment except on one side. Its walls have two small windows or openings which have been called doorways, and are of a single story in height. This tower was apparently ceremonial in character.

It is instructive to mention that remains of a fire hole containing wood ashes occur in the floor on one side of this room, and that the walls are pierced with several small holes opening at an angle. Only foundations remain of the other circular room. It was situated on the south side of the open space containing kiva H and formed a bastion at the north end of the front wall. The floor of this room was wholly covered with fallen débris and its ground plan was wholly concealed when the excavations began; it was only with considerable difficulty that the foundation walls could be traced.

---

[a] It has no doubt occurred to others, as to the author, that the number of Spruce-tree House kivas is a multiple of four, the number of horizontal cardinal points. Later it may be found that there is some connection between them and world-quarter clan ownership, or it may be that the agreement in numbers is purely a coincidence,

CEREMONIAL ROOM OTHER THAN KIVA

While the circular subterranean rooms above mentioned are believed to be the most common ceremonial chambers, there are others in the cliff-dwellings which were undoubtedly used for similar purposes. One of these, designated room 12, adjoins the mortuary room (11) and opens on the plaza C, D. In some respects the form of this room is similar to an " estufa of singular construction " described and figured in Nordenskiöld's account of Cliff Palace. Certain distinctive characters of this room separate it on one side from a kiva and on the other from a dwelling. In the first place, it lacks the circular form and subterranean site. The six pedestals which universally support the roofs are likewise absent. In fact they are not needed because in this room the top of the cave serves as the roof. A bank extends around three sides of the room, the fourth side being the perpendicular wall of the cliff. In the southeast corner is an opening, which recalls that in the " estufa of singular construction " described by Nordenskiöld.[a]

MORTUARY ROOM

Room 9 may be designated a mortuary room from the fact that at least four human skeletons and accompanying offerings have been found in its floor. Three of those, excavated several years ago, were said to have been infants; the skull of one of these was figured and described by Prof. G. Retzius, in Nordenskiöld's memoir. The skeleton found by the author was that of an adult and was accompanied by mortuary offerings. The skull and some of the larger bones were well preserved.[b] Evidently the doorway of this room had been walled up and there are indications that the burials took place at intervals, the last occurring before the desertion of the village.

The presence of burials in the floors of rooms in Spruce-tree House was to be expected, as the practice of thus disposing of the dead was known from other ruins of the Park, but it has not been pointed out that we have in this region good evidence of several successive interments in the same room. The existence of this intramural burial room in the south end of the ruin is one of the facts that can be adduced pointing to the conclusion that this part of the ruin is very old.

SMALL LEDGE-HOUSES

Not far from the Spruce-tree House, situated in the same canyon, there are small one-room houses perched on narrow ledges situated generally a little higher than the cave containing the main ruin.

---

[a] The Cliff Dwellers of the Mesa Verde, p. 63.

[b] In clearing the kivas several fragments of human bones and skulls were found by the author. The horizontal passageways, called ventilators, of four of the kivas furnished a single broken skull each, which had not been buried with care.

Although it is difficult to enter some of these houses, members of the author's party visited all of them, and two of the workmen slept in a small ledge-house on the west side of the canyon. Except in rare cases these smaller houses can not be considered dwellings; they may have been used for storage, although it is more than likely that they were resorted to by priests when they wished to pray for rain or to perform certain ceremonies. The ledge-houses form a distinct type of ruin; they are rarely multiple-chambered and therefore are not capacious enough for more than one family.

STAIRWAYS

There are two or three old stairway trails in the neighborhood of Spruce-tree House. These consist of a succession of holes for hands and feet, or of a series of pits cut in the face of the cliff at convenient distances. One of these ancient trails is situated on the west side of the canyon not far from the modern trail to the spring; the other lies on the east side a few feet north of the ruin. Both of these trails were appropriately labeled for the convenience of future visitors. There is still another ancient trail along the east canyon wall south of the ruin. Although all these trails are somewhat obscure, it is hoped that they can be readily found by means of the labels posted near them.

REFUSE-HEAPS

In the rear of the buildings are two large open spaces which, from their positions relative to the main street, may be called the northern and southern refuse-heaps. They merit more than passing consideration. The former, being the larger, has not yet been thoroughly cleared out, although pretty well dug over before the repair work was begun. The author completely cleared out the southern refuse-heap and excavated to its floor.[a]

The southern recess opens directly into the main street and is flooded with light. Its floor is covered with large fragments of rock that have fallen from the cliff above. The spaces between these bowlders were filled with débris and the bowlders themselves were covered with the same accumulations the removal of which was no small task.

MINOR ANTIQUITIES

The rooms and refuse-heaps of Spruce-tree House had been pretty thoroughly ransacked for specimens by those who preceded the author, so that few minor antiquities were expected to come to light in the excavation and repair work. Notwithstanding this, however, a fair col-

---

[a] From the great amount of bird-lime and bones in these heaps it has been supposed that turkeys were domesticated and kept in these places.

lection, containing some unique specimens and many representative objects, was made, and is now in the National Museum where it will be preserved and be accessible to all students. Considering the fact that most of the specimens previously abstracted from this ruin have been scattered in all directions and are now in many hands, it is doubtful whether a collection of any considerable size from Sprucetree House exists in any other public museum. In order to render this account more comprehensive, references are made in the following pages to objects from Spruce-tree House elsewhere described, now in other collections. These references, quoted from Nordenskiöld, the only writer on this subject, are as follows:

Plate xviii: 2. a and b. Strongly flattened cranium of a child. Found in a room in Sprucetree House.

Plate xxxiv: 4. Stone axe of porphyrite. Sprucetree House.

Plate xxxv: 2. Rough-hewn stone axe of quartzite. Sprucetree House.

Plate xxxix: 6. Implement of black slate. Form peculiar (see the text). Found in Sprucetree House.

[In the text the last-mentioned specimen is again referred to, as follows:]

I have still to mention a number of stone implements the use of which is unknown to me, first some large (15–30 cm.), flat, and rather thick stones of irregular shape and much worn at the edges (Pl. xxxix: 4, 5), second a singular object consisting of a thin slab of black slate, and presenting the appearance shown in Pl. xxxix: 6. My collection contains only one such implement, but among the objects in Wetherill's possession I saw several. They are all of exactly the same shape and of almost the same size. I cannot say in what manner this slab of slate was employed. Perhaps it is a last for the plaiting of sandals or the cutting of moccasins. In size it corresponds pretty nearly to the foot of an adult.

Plate xl: 5. Several *ulnæ* and *radii* of birds (turkeys) tied on a buckskin string and probably used as an amulet. Found in Sprucetree House.

Plate xliii: 6. Bundle of 19 sticks of hard wood, probably employed in some kind of knitting or crochet work. The pins are pointed at one end, blunt at the other, and black with wear. They are held together by a narrow band of yucca. Found in Sprucetree House.

Plate xliv: 2. Similar to the preceding basket, but smaller. Found in Sprucetree House. . . .

[The "preceding basket" is thus described in explanation of the figure (Pl. xliv: 1):] Basket of woven yucca in two different colors, a neat pattern being thus attained. The strips of yucca running in a vertical direction are of the natural yellowish brown, the others (in horizontal direction) darker. . . .

Plate xlv: 1(95) and 2(663): Small baskets of yucca, of plain colour and of handsomely plaited pattern. Found: 1 in ruin 9, 2 in Sprucetree House.

Plate xlviii: 4(674). Mat of plaited reeds, originally 1.2×1.2 m., but damaged in transportation. Found in Sprucetree House.

It appears from the foregoing that the following specimens have been described and figured by Nordenskiöld, from Spruce-tree House: (1) A child's skull; (2) 2 stone axes; (3) a slab of black slate; (4) several bird bones used for amulet; (5) bundle of sticks; (6) 2 small baskets; (7) a plaited mat.

In addition to the specimens above referred to, the majority of which are duplicated in the author's collection, no objects from Spruce-tree House are known to have been described or figured elsewhere, so that there are embraced in the present account practically all printed references to known material from this ruin. But there is no doubt that other specimens as yet unmentioned in print still exist in public collections in Colorado, and later these also may be described and figured. From the nature of the author's excavations and method of collecting, little hope remains that additional specimens may be obtained from rooms in Spruce-tree House, but the northern refuse-heap situated at the back of the cavern may yet yield a few good objects. This still awaits complete scientific excavation.

The author's collection from Spruce-tree House, the choice specimens of which are now in the National Museum, numbers several hundred objects. All the duplicates and heavy specimens, about equal in number to the lighter ones, were left at the ruin where they are available for future study. These are mostly stone mauls, metates and large grinding implements, and broken bowls and vases. The absence from Spruce-tree House of certain characteristic objects widely distributed among Southwestern ruins is regarded as worthy of comment. It will be noticed in looking over the author's collection that there are no specimens of marine shells, or of turquoise ornaments or obsidian flakes, from the excavations made at Spruce-tree House. This fact is significant, meaning either that the former inhabitants of this village were ignorant of these objects or that the excavators failed to find what may have existed. The author accepts the former explanation, that these objects were not in use by the inhabitants of Spruce-tree House, their ignorance of them having been due mainly to their restricted commercial dealings with their neighbors.

Obsidian, one of the rarest stones in the cliff-dwellings of the Mesa Verde, as a rule is characteristic of very old ruins and occurs in those having kivas of the round type, to the south and west of that place.

It is said that turquoise has been found in the Mesa Verde ruins. The author has seen a beautiful bird mosaic with inlaid turquoise from one of the ruins near Cortez in Montezuma valley. This specimen is made of hematite with turquoise eyes and neckband of the same material; the feathers are represented by stripes of inlaid turquoise. Also inlaid in turquoise in the back is an hour-glass figure, recalling designs drawn in outline on ancient pottery.

The absence of bracelets, armlets, and finger rings of sea shells, objects so numerous in the ruins along the Little Colorado and the Gila, may be explained by lack of trade, due to culture isolation.

The people of Mesa Verde appear not to have come in contact with tribes who traded these shells, consequently they never obtained them. The absence of culture connection in this direction tells in favor of the theory that the ancestors of the Mesa Verde people did not come from the southwest or the west, where shells are so abundant. Although not proving much either way by itself, this theory, when taken with other facts which admit of the same interpretation, is significant. The inhabitants of Spruce-tree House (the same is true of the other Mesa Verde people) had an extremely narrow mental horizon. They obtained little in trade from their neighbors and were quite unconscious of the extent of the culture of which they were representatives.

POTTERY

The women of Spruce-tree House were expert potters and decorated their wares in a simple but artistic manner. Until we have more material it would be gratuitous to assume that the ceramic art objects of all the Mesa Verde ruins are identical in texture, colors, and symbolism, and the only way to determine how great are the variations, if any, would be to make an accurate comparative study of pottery from different localities. Thus far the quantity of material available does not justify comparison even of the ruins of this mesa, but there is a good beginning of a collection from Spruce-tree House. The custom of placing in graves offerings of food for the dead has preserved several good bowls, and although whole pieces are rare fragments are found in abundance. Eighteen earthenware vessels, including those repaired and restored from fragments, rewarded the author's excavations at Spruce-tree House. Some of these vessels bear a rare and beautiful symbolism which is quite different from that known from Arizona. The few plates (16–20) here given to illustrate these symbols are offered more as a basis for future study and comparisons than as an exhaustive representation of ceramics from one ruin.

The number and variety of pieces of pottery figured from the Mesa Verde cliff-dwellings have not been great. An examination of Nordenskiöld's memoir reveals the fact that he represents about 50 specimens of pottery; several of these were obtained by purchase, and others came from Chelly canyon, the pottery of which is strikingly like that of Mesa Verde. The majority of specimens obtained by Nordenskiöld's excavations were from Step House, not a single ceramic object from Spruce-tree House being figured. So far as the author can ascertain, the ceramic specimens here considered are the first representatives of this art from Spruce-tree House that have been described or figured, but there may be many other specimens from this locality awaiting description and it is to be hoped that some day these may be made known to the scientific world.

FORMS

Every form of pottery represented by Nordenskiöld, with the exception of that which he styles a "lamp-shaped" vessel and of certain platter forms with indentations, occurs in the collection here considered.

Nordenskiöld figures a jar provided with a lid, both sides of which are shown.[a] It would seem that this lid (fig. 1),[b] unlike those provided with knobs, found by the author, had two holes near the center. The decoration on the top of the lid of one of the author's specimens resembles that figured by Nordenskiöld, but other specimens differ from his as shown in figure 1. The specimens having raised lips and lids are perforated in the edges of the openings, with one or more holes for strings or handles. As bowls of this form are found in sacred rooms they would seem to have been connected

FIG. 1. Lid of jar.

with worship. The author believes that they served the same purposes as the netted gourds of the Hopi. Most of the ceramic objects in Spruce-tree House were in fragments when found.[c] Some of these objects have been repaired and it is remarkable that so much good material for the study of the symbolism has been obtained in this way.

Black-and-white ware is the most common and the characteristic painted pottery, but fragmentary specimens of a reddish ware occur. One peculiarity in the lips of food bowls from Spruce-tree House (pls. 16–18) is that their rims are flat, instead of rounded as in more western prehistoric ruins, like Sikyatki. Food bowls are rarely concave at the base.

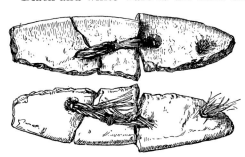

FIG. 2. Repaired pottery.

No fragments of glazed pottery were found, although the surfaces of some species were very smooth and glossy from constant rubbing with smoothing stones. Several pieces of pottery were unequally fired, so that a vitreous mass, or blotch, was evident on one side. Smooth vessels and those made of coiled ware, which were covered with soot from fires, were evidently used in cooking.

Several specimens showed evidences of having been broken and

[a] See The Cliff Dwellers of the Mesa Verde, pls. xxviii, xxix : 7.

[b] The text figures which appear in this paper were drawn from nature by Mrs. M. W. Gill, of Forest Glen, Md.

[c] The author is greatly indebted to Mr. A. V. Kidder for aid in sorting and labeling the fragments of pottery. Without his assistance in the field it would have been impossible to repair many of these specimens.

afterwards mended by the owners (fig. 2); holes were drilled near the line of fracture and the two parts tied together; even the yucca strings still remain in the holes, showing where fragments were united. In figure 3 there is represented a fragment of a handle of an amphora on which is tied a tightly-woven cord.

FIG. 3. Handle with attached cord.

Not a very great variety of pottery forms was brought to light in the operations at Spruce-tree House. Those that were found are essentially the types common throughout the Southwest, and may be classified as follows: (1) Large jars, or ollas; (2) flat food bowls; (3) cups and mugs; (4) ladles or dippers (fig. 4); (5) canteens; (6) globular bowls. An exceptional form is a globular bowl with a raised lip like a sugar bowl (pl. 19, *f*). This form is never seen in other prehistoric ruins.

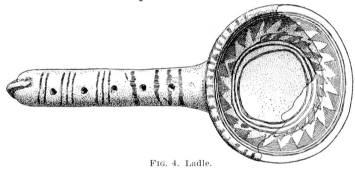

FIG. 4. Ladle.

STRUCTURE

Classified by structure, the pottery found in the Spruce-tree House ruin falls into two groups, coiled ware and smooth ware, the latter either with or without decoration. The white ware has black decorations.

The bases of the mugs (pl. 19) from Spruce-tree House, like those from other Mesa Verde ruins, have a greater diameter than the lips. These mugs are tall and their handles are of generous size. One of the mugs found in this ruin has a **T**-shaped hole in its handle (fig. 5), recalling in this particular a mug collected in 1895 by the author at Awatobi, a Hopi ruin.

The most beautiful specimen of canteen found at Spruce-tree House is here shown in plate 20.

FIG. 5. Handle of mug.

The coiled ware of Spruce-tree House, as of all the Mesa Verde ruins, is somewhat finer than the coiled ware of Sikyatki. Although no complete specimen was found, many fragments were collected, some of which are of great size. This kind of ware was apparently the most abundant and also the most fragile. As a rule these vessels show marks of fire, soot, or smoke on the outside, and were evidently used as cooking vessels. On account of their fragile character they could not have been used for carrying water, for, with one or two exceptions, they would not be equal to the strain. In decoration of coiled ware the women of Spruce-tree House resorted to an ingenious modification of the coils, making triangular figures, spirals, or crosses in relief, which were usually affixed to the necks of the vessels.

The symbolism on the pottery of Spruce-tree House is essentially that of a cliff-dwelling culture, being simple in general characters. Although it has many affinities with the archaic symbols of the Pueblos, it has not the same complexity. The reason for this can be readily traced to that same environmental influence which caused the communities to seek the cliffs for protection. The very isolation of the Mesa Verde cliff-dwellings prevented the influx of new ideas and consequently the adoption of new symbols to represent them. Secure in their cliffs, the inhabitants were not subject to the invasion of strange clans nor could new customs be introduced, so that conservatism ruled their art as well as their life in general. Only simple symbols were present because there was no outside stimulus or competition to make them complex.

On classification of Spruce-tree House pottery according to technique, irrespective of its form, two divisions appear: (1) Coiled ware showing the coils externally, and (2) smooth ware with or without decorations. Structurally both divisions are the same, although their outward appearance is different.

The smooth ware may be decorated with incised lines or pits, but is painted often in one color. All the decorated vessels obtained by the author at Spruce-tree House belong to what is called black-and-white ware, by which is meant pottery having a thin white slip covering the whole surface upon which black pictures are painted. Occasionally fragments of a reddish brown cup were found, while red ware bearing white decorative figures was recovered from the Mesa Verde; but none of these are ascribed to Spruce-tree House or were collected by the author. The general geographical distribution of this black-and-white ware, not taking into account sporadic examples, is about the same as that of the circular kivas, but it is also found where circular kivas are unknown, as in the upper part of the valley of the Little Colorado.

The black-and-white ware of modern pueblos, as Zuñi and Hano, the latter the Tewan pueblo among the Hopi, is of late introduction from the Rio Grande; prehistoric Zuñi ware is unlike that of modern

Zuñi, being practically identical in character with that of the other ancient pueblos of the Little Colorado and its tributaries.

As a rule, the decoration on pottery from Spruce-tree House is simple, being composed mainly of geometrical patterns. Life forms are rare, when present consisting chiefly of birds or rude figures of mammals

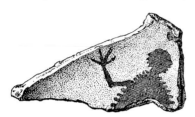

FIG. 6. Fragment of pottery.

painted on the outside of food bowls (fig. 6). The geometrical figures are principally rectilinear, there being a great paucity of spirals and curved lines. The tendency to arrange rows of dots along straight lines is marked in Mesa Verde pottery and occurs also in dados of house walls. There are many examples of stepped or terraced figures which are so arranged in pairs that the spaces between the terraces form zigzag bands, as shown in figure 7. A band extending from the upper left hand, to the lower right hand, angle of the rectangle that incloses the two terraced figures, may be designated a sinistral, and when at right angles a dextral, terraced figure (fig. 8). Specimens from Spruce-tree House show considerable modification in these two types.

FIG. 7. Zigzag ornament.

With exception of the terrace the triangle (fig. 9) is possibly the most common geometrical decoration on Spruce-tree House pottery.

FIG. 8. Sinistral and dextral stepped figures.

Most of the triangles may be bases of terraced figures, for by cutting notches on the longer sides of these triangles, sinistral or dextral stepped figures (as the case may be) result.

The triangles may be placed in a row, united in hourglass forms, or distributed in other ways. These triangles may be equilateral or one of the angles may be very acute. Although the possibilities of triangle combinations are almost innumerable the different forms can be readily recognized. The dot is a common form of decoration, and parallel lines also are much used. Many bowls are decorated with hachure, and with line ornaments mostly rectilinear.

FIG. 9. Triangle ornament.

The volute plays a part, although not a conspicuous one, in Spruce-tree House pottery decoration. Simple volutes are of two kinds, one in which the figure-coils follow the direction of the hands of the clock (dextral); the other, in which they take an opposite direction (sinistral). The outer end of the volute may terminate in a triangle or other figure, which may be notched, serrated, or otherwise modified. A compound sinistral volute is one which is sinistral until it reaches the center, when it turns into a dextral volute extending to the periphery. The compound dextral volute is exactly the reverse of the last-mentioned, starting as dextral and ending as sinistral. If, as frequently happens, there is a break in the lines at the middle, the figure may be called a broken compound volute. Two volutes having different axes are known as a composite volute, sinistral or dextral as the case may be.

The meander (fig. 10) is also important in Spruce-tree House or Mesa Verde pottery decoration. The form of meander homologous to the volute may be classified in the same terms as the volute, into (1) simple sinistral meander; (2) simple dextral meander; (3) compound sinistral meander; (4) compound dextral meander; and (5) composite meander. These meanders, like the volutes, may be accompanied by parallel lines or by rows of dots enlarged, serrated, notched, or otherwise modified.

FIG. 10. Meander.

In some beautiful specimens a form of hachure, or combination of many parallel lines with spirals and meanders, is introduced in a very effective way. This kind of decoration is very rare on old Hopi (Sikyatki) pottery, but is common on late Zuñi and Hano ceramics, both of which are probably derived from the Rio Grande region.

Lines, straight or zigzag, constitute important elements in Spruce-tree House pottery decoration. These may be either parallel, or crossed so as to form reticulated areas.

Along these lines rows of dots or of triangular enlargements may be introduced. The latter may be simply serrations, dentations, or triangles of considerable size, sometimes bent over, resembling pointed bands.

Curved figures are rarely used, but such as are found are characteristic. Concentric rings, with or without central dots, are not uncommon.

Rectangles apparently follow the same general rules as circles, and are also sometimes simple, with or without central dots.

The triangle is much more common as a decorative motive than the circle or the rectangle, variety being brought about by the difference in length of the sides. The hourglass formed by two triangles with one angle of each united is common. The quail's-head design, or triangle having two parallel marks on an extension at one angle, is not as common as on Little Colorado pottery and that from the Gila valley.

As in all ceramics from the San Juan area, the stepped figures are most abundant. There are two types of stepped figures, the sinistral and the dextral, according as the steps pass from left to right or vice versa. The color of the two stepped figures may be black, or one or both may have secondary ornamentation in forms of hachure or network. One may be solid black, the other filled in with lines.

In addition to the above-mentioned geometrical figures, the S-shaped design is common; when doubled, this forms the cross called swastika. The S figure is of course generally curved but may be angular, in which case the cross is more evident. One bowl has the S figure on the outside. All of the above-mentioned designs admit of variations and two or more are often combined in Spruce-tree House pottery, which is practically the same in type as that of the whole Mesa Verde region.

CERAMIC AREAS

While it is yet too early in our study of prehistoric pueblo culture to make or define subcultural areas, it is possible to recognize provisionally certain areas having features in common, which differ from other areas.[a] It has already been shown that the form of the subterranean ceremonial room can be used as a basis of classification. If pottery symbols are taken as the basis, it will be found that there are at least two great subsections in the pueblo country coinciding with the two divisions recognized as the result of study of the form of sacred rooms—the northeastern and the southwestern region or, for brevity, the northern and the southern area. In the former region lie, besides the Mesa Verde and the San Juan valley, Chaco and Chelly canyons; in the latter, the ruins of " great houses " along the Gila and Salt rivers.

From these two centers radiated in ancient times two types of pottery symbols expressive of two distinct cultures, each ceremonially distinct and, architecturally speaking, characteristic. The line of junction of the influences of these two subcultural areas practically follows the Little Colorado river, the valley of which is the site of a third ceramic subculture area; this is mixed, being related on one side to the northern, on the other to the southern, region. The course of this river and its tributaries has determined a trail of migration, which in turn has spread this intermingled ceramic art far and wide. The geographical features of the Little Colorado basin have prevented the evolution of characteristic ceramic culture in any part of the region.

---

[a] The classification into cavate houses, cliff-dwellings, and pueblos is based on form.

Using color and symbolism of pottery as a basis of classification, the author has provisionally divided the sedentary people of the Southwest into the following divisions, or has recognized the following ceramic areas: (1) Hopi area, including the wonderful ware of Sikyatki, Awatobi, and the ruins on Antelope mesa, at old Mishongnovi, Shumopavi and neighboring ruins; (2) Casa Grande area; (3) San Juan area, including Mesa Verde, Chaco canyon, Chelly canyon as far west as St. George, Utah, and Navaho mountain, Arizona; (4) Little Colorado area, including Zuñi. The pottery of Casas Grandes in Chihuahua is allied in colors but not in symbols to old Hopi ware. So little is known of the old Piros ceramics and of the pottery from all ruins east of the Rio Grande, that they are not yet classified. The ceramics from the region west of the Rio Grande are related to the San Juan and Chaco areas.

The Spruce-tree House pottery belongs to the San Juan area, having some resemblance and relationship to that from the lower course of the Little Colorado. It is markedly different from the pottery of the Hopi area and has only the most distant resemblance to that from Casas Grandes.[a]

HOPI AREA

The Hopi area is well distinguished by specialized symbols which are not duplicated elsewhere in the pueblo area. Among these may be mentioned the symbol for the feather, and a band representing the sky with design of a mythic bird attached. As almost all pueblo symbols, ancient and modern, are represented on old Hopi ware, and in addition other designs peculiar to it, the logical conclusion is that these Hopi symbols are specialized in origin.

The evolution of a ceramic area in the neighborhood of the modern Hopi mesas is due to special causes, and points to a long residence in that locality. It would seem from traditions that the earliest Hopi people came from the east, and that the development of a purely Hopi ceramic culture in the region now occupied by this people took place before any great change due to southern immigration had occurred. The entrance of Patki and other clans from the south strongly affected the old Hopi culture, which was purest in Sikyatki, but even there it remained distinctive. The advent of the eastern clans in large numbers after the great rebellion in 1680, especially of the Tanoan families about 1710, radically changed the symbolism, making modern Hopi ware completely eastern in this respect. The old symbolism, the germ of which was eastern, as shown by the characters employed, almost completely vanished, being replaced by an introduced symbolism.

---

[a] The above classification coincides in some respects with that obtained by using the forms of ceremonial rooms as the basis.

In order scientifically to appreciate the bearing on the migration of clans, of symbolism on pottery, we must bear in mind that a radical difference in such symbolism as has taken place at the Hopi villages may have occurred elsewhere as well, although there is no evidence of a change of this kind having occurred at Spruce-tree House.

The author includes under Hopi ware that found at the Hopi ruins Sikyatki, Shumopavi, and Awatobi, the collection from the first-named being typical. Some confusion has been introduced by others into the study of old Hopi ware by including in it, under the name " Tusayan pottery," the white-and-black ware of the Chelly canyon.[a] There is a close resemblance between the pottery of Chelly canyon and that of Mesa Verde, but only the most distant relationship between true Hopi ware and that of Chelly canyon. The latter belong in fact to two distinct areas, and differ in color, symbolism, and general characters. In so far as the Hopi ware shares its symbolism with the other geographical areas of the eastern region, to the same extent there is kinship in culture. In more distant ruins the pottery contains a greater admixture of symbols foreign to Mesa Verde. These differences are due no doubt to incorporation of other clans.

The subceramic area in which the Mesa Verde ruins lie embraces the valleys of the San Juan and its tributaries, Chelly canyon, Chaco canyon, and probably the ruins along the Rio Grande, on both sides of the river. Whether the Chaco or the Mesa Verde region is the geographical center of this subarea, or not, can not be determined, but the indications are that the Mesa Verde is on its northern border. Along the southwestern and western borders the culture of this area mingles with that of the subcultural area adjoining on the south, the resultant symbolism being consequently more complex. The ceramic ware of ruins of the Mesa Verde is little affected by outside and diverse influences, while, on the contrary, similar ware found along the western and southern borders of the subcultural area has been much modified by the influence of the neighboring region.

LITTLE COLORADO AREA

Although the decoration on pottery from Spruce-tree House embraces some symbols in common with that of the ruins along the Little Colorado, including prehistoric Zuñi, there is evidence of a mingling of the two ceramic types which is believed to have originated in the Gila basin. The resemblance in the pottery of these regions is greater near the sources of the Little Colorado, differences increasing as one descends the river. At Homolobi (near Winslow) and Chev-

---

[a] Of 40 pieces of pottery called "Tusayan," figured in Professor Holmes' Pottery of the Pueblo Area (*Second Annual Report of the Bureau of Ethnology*), all but three or possibly four came from Chelly canyon and belong to the San Juan rather than to the Hopi ware. Black-and-white pottery is very rare in collections of old Hopi ware, but is most abundant in the cliff-houses of Chelly canyon and the Mesa Verde ruins.

lon, where the pottery is half northern and half southern in type, these differences have almost disappeared.

This is what might be expected theoretically, and is in accordance with legends of the Hopi, for the Little Colorado ruins are more modern than the round-kiva culture of Chaco canyon and Mesa Verde, and than the square-ceremonial-house culture of the Gila. The indications are that symbolism of the Little Colorado ruins is a composite, representative in about equal proportions of the two subcultures of the Southwest.[a]

As confirmatory of this suggested dual origin we find that the symbolism of pottery from ruins near the source of the Little Colorado is identical with that of the Salt, the Verde, and the Tonto basins, from which their inhabitants originally came in larger numbers than from the Rio Grande. In the ruins of the upper Salt and Gila the pottery is more like that of the neighboring sources of the Little Colorado because of interchanges. On the other hand, the ancient Hopi, being more isolated than other Pueblos, especially those on the Little Colorado, developed a ceramic art peculiar to themselves. Their pottery is different from that of the Little Colorado, the upper Gila and its tributary, the Salt, and the San Juan including the Mesa Verde.

The Zuñi valley, lying practically in the pathway of culture migration or about midway between the northern and southern subceramic areas, had no distinctive ancient pottery. Its ancient pottery is not greatly unlike that of Homolobi near Winslow but has been influenced about equally by the northern and the southern type. Whatever originality in culture symbols developed in the Zuñi valley was immediately merged with others and spread over a large area.[b]

MESA VERDE AREA

While there are several subdivisions in the eastern subcultural area, that in which the Mesa Verde ruins are situated is distinctive. The area embraces the ruins in the Montezuma valley and those of Chelly canyon, and the San Juan ruins as far as Navaho mountain, including also the Chaco and the Canyon Largo ruins. Probably the pottery of some of the ruins east of the Rio Grande will be found to belong to the same type. That of the Hopi ceramic area, the so-called "Tusayan," exclusive of Chelly canyon, is distinct from all others. The pottery of the Gila subculture area is likewise distinctive but its influence made its way up the Verde and the Tonto and was potent across the mountains, in the Little Colorado basin.

---

[a] The pottery from ruins in the Little Colorado basin, from Wukoki at Black Falls to the Great Colorado, is more closely allied to that of the drainage of the San Juan and its tributaries.

[b] There is of course very little ancient Zuñi ware in museums, but such as we have justifies the conclusion stated above.

Its influence is likewise strong in the White Mountain ruins and on the Tularosa, and around the sources of the Gila and Salt rivers.

An examination of the decoration of pottery from Spruce-tree House fails to reveal a single specimen with the well known broken encircling line called "the line of life." As this feature is absent from pottery from all the Mesa Verde ruins it may be said provisionally that the ancient potters of this region were unfamiliar with it.

This apparently insignificant characteristic is present, however, in all the pottery directly influenced by the culture of the southwestern subceramic area. It occurs in pottery from the Gila and the Salt River ruins, in the Hopi area, and along the Little Colorado, including the Zuñi valley, and elsewhere. Until recorded from the northeastern subceramic area, "the line of life" may be considered a peculiarity of ceramics of the Gila subarea or of the pottery influenced by its culture.

Among the restored food bowls from Spruce-tree House, having characteristic symbols, may be mentioned that represented in plate 16, d, d', which has on the interior surface a triangular design with curved appendages to each angle. The triangular arrangement of designs on the interior surface of food bowls is not uncommon in the Mesa Verde pottery.

Another food bowl has two unusual designs on the interior surface, as shown in plate 18, c, c'. The meaning of this rare symbolism is unknown.

In plates 16–19 are represented some of the most characteristic symbols on the restored pottery.

The outer surfaces of many food bowls are elaborately decorated with designs as shown, while the rims in most cases are dotted.

STONE IMPLEMENTS

Stone implements from Spruce-tree House include axes, mauls, stone hammers, and grinding stones, in addition to other objects of unknown uses. As a rule these stone implements are rudely made, although some of them are as fine as any known from the Southwest. It is but natural that these implements should have been manufactured from more compact and harder rock than that of which the walls of the buildings were constructed. Apparently these objects were not picked up in the neighborhood but brought to the site of the ruin from a great distance.

AXES

The author collected several stone axes (pl. 21 and fig. 11) from Spruce-tree House, some of which (a–f) are fine specimens. These are all of the same general type, sharpened at one end and blunt at the opposite end, with a groove midway for attachment of the handle. In no case is there a ridge bordering this groove which in one specimen (pl. 21, *g*) is partially duplicated.

One ax has a cutting edge at each end, while another (fig. 12) has the handle still attached, recalling the two specimens figured by Nordenskiöld.

FIG. 11. Stone axes.

Among the objects of stone taken from Spruce-tree House are several similar to those called by the Hopi *tcamahias* (pl. 21, *h*). These implements are as a rule long, with smooth surfaces; they are sharpened at one end and pointed at the opposite end. Generally they have no groove for the attachment of a handle; in one instance, however, there is an indentation on opposite borders. The use of these objects is unknown; they may have been axes or planting implements.

Stone objects of precisely the same type are highly prized by the Hopi and play important parts in their ceremonials. A number of these objects are arranged about the sand picture of the Antelope altar in the Snake dance at Walpi.[a]

Similar specimens are attached by the Hopi to their most sacred palladium, called the *tiponi*, or badge of office of the chief of a priest-

Fig. 12. Stone ax with handle.

hood. The tiponi of the Antelope society has one of these projecting from its top. The meaning of this association may be even greater than at first would be suspected, for according to legends the Snake family, which is the guardian of the fetishes used in the snake ceremonies, originally lived at Tokonabi, near Navaho mountain, at the mouth of the San Juan river. The culture of the ancient inhabitants of the ruins at that place was not very different from that of the people of the Mesa Verde.

GRINDING STONES

Both pestles and hand stones used in grinding maize were excavated, the latter in considerable numbers. There were found also many stone slabs having rounded depressions, or pits, on opposite sides, evidently similar to those now used by the Hopi in grinding the paints for their ceremonials. In some places peckings or grooves in the surfaces of the rocks show where these grinding stones were used, and perhaps flattened to the desired plane. These grinding places are found in the plazas, on the sides of the cave back of the village, and elsewhere. A number of these grooves in a lower ledge of rock at the spring indicate that this was a favorite spot for shaping the hand grinders, possibly for grinding corn or other seeds.

The hand stones are of several types: (1) Polygonal, having corners somewhat worn, but flat on both sides, and having grooves on opposite edges to insure a firm hold for the hand; (2) convex on one

---

[a] Snake Ceremonials at Walpi, in *Journal of American Archæology and Ethnology,* IV, 1894.

face and flat on the opposite; (3) having two faces on each side, separated by a sharp ridge. The third type represents apparently the last stage in the life of a grinding stone the surfaces of which have been worn to this shape by constant use.

Several flat stones, each having a slight depression on one side, were found to be covered with pigments of various colors, which were ground on their surfaces by means of conical stones, as shown in figure 13. Two rectangular flat stones (pl. 21, *i*, *j*) with finely polished surfaces and rounded edges have a notch on the rim. Their use is unknown. Nordenskiöld refers to similar stones as "moccasin lasts," but there seems no valid reason thus to identify these objects except that they have the general form—although larger—of the sole of the foot. The Spruce-tree House aborigines wore sandals and had no need for lasts. Moreover, so far as known, the Pueblo Indians never made use of an object of this kind in fashioning their moccasins.

POUNDING STONES

In the course of the excavations a large number of stones having pits in the sides were exhumed, but these are so heavy that they were not sent to Washington. Several of these stones are cubical in form and have lateral pits, one on each of four faces. Some are thick, while others are thin and sharpened at the end like an ax. These stones are probably the mauls with which the masons

FIG. 13. Stone pigment-grinder.

dressed the rocks used in the construction of the buildings. With such mauls the surfaces of the floors of some ceremonial rooms were cut down several inches below the original level. Some of the pounding stones resemble in a measure the grinding stones, but in them pits replace grooves commonly found in the edge of the latter.

Corn was usually ground on flat stones called *metates* which were found in considerable numbers. These metates commonly show wear on one or both surfaces, and a few specimens have a ridge on each border resulting from the wearing down of the middle of the stone.

CYLINDER OF POLISHED HEMATITE

Among the objects from the ruins of Mesa Verde figured by Nordenskiöld is one designated a "cylinder of polished hematite, perhaps a fetish." Another stone cylinder closely resembling this was found by the present author at Spruce-tree House. This object closely resembles a bead, but as the author has seen similar stones used on Hopi altars, especially on the altar to the cardinal points, he is inclined to accept the identification suggested by Nordenskiöld. On altars to the cardinal points small stones of different shapes and colors are arranged near ears of corn surrounding a medicine bowl. As black is the symbolic color of the underworld, a stone of this color is found on the black ear of corn representing the nadir. If this cylinder is a fetish it may have been somewhat similarly used.

FIG. 14. Fragment of basket.

BASKETRY

Not a single entire basket was found, although a few fragments of baskets made of woven rushes or osiers were obtained (fig. 14). It would appear, however, from a fine basket figured by Nordenskiöld, which he ascribes to Spruce-tree House and from other known specimens, figured and unfigured, that the Mesa Verde people were skillful basket makers. None of the fragments obtained by the author, and the same holds true regarding the basket figured by Nordenskiöld, are decorated.

WOODEN OBJECTS

Few objects made of wood were obtained at Spruce-tree House, but those which were found are well made and reveal the existence of interesting aboriginal customs. Wooden objects closely resembling some of these were used until a few years ago by the Hopi and other Pueblo tribes.

STICKS TIED TOGETHER

Among the wooden objects found are many perforated sticks tied together by strings. This specimen (fig. 15) is not complete, but

FIG. 15. Sticks tied together.

enough remains to show that it is not unlike the covering in which the Hopi bride rolls her wedding blankets. From the place where the object was found, it appears that the dead were wrapped in coverings of this kind. Although the specimen is much damaged, it is not difficult to make out from the remaining fragment the mode of construction of the object.

SLABS

Nordenskiöld figures a wooden object of rectangular shape, slightly concave on one side and more or less worn on the edges. Two similar

FIG. 16. Wooden slab.

wooden slabs (fig. 16) were found at Spruce-tree House. The objects occasioned much speculation, as their meaning is unknown. It has been suggested they are cradle-boards, a conjecture which, in view of the fact that similar specimens are sometimes found in child burials, is plausible. In this interpretation the holes which occur on the sides may have served for attachment of blankets or hoops. These boards, it may be said, are small even for the most diminutive Indian baby.

Another suggestion not without merit is that these boards are priest's badges and were once carried in the hands suspended by strings tied to the holes in their edges.

Still another theory identifies them as parts of head dresses called tablets, worn in what the Pueblos call a *tablita* dance.

The upright portions of some of the Hopi altars have similar wooden slabs painted with symbolic figures and tied together. Altars having slabs of the same description are used in ceremonials of certain Tewan clans living in New Mexico.

SPINDLES

There were found at Spruce-tree House a complete spindle with stick and whorl (fig. 17), and a whorl without the spindle, both of which are practically identical in type with the spinning apparatus of the Hopi Indians. When in use this spindle was made to revolve by rubbing it on the thigh with one hand, while the other held the unspun cotton, the fiber being wound on one end of the spindle. This implement affords still another indication that the arts of the people of Spruce-tree House were similar to those still practised by the Pueblos,

FIG. 17. Spindle and whorl.

PLANTING-STICKS.

A few sticks which resemble those used by the Hopi as dibbles were collected at Spruce-tree House. These measure several feet in length; they are flat at one end, while the opposite end is pointed and rubbed down to a sharp edge. Some of these implements were slightly bent at one extremity.

MISCELLANEOUS OBJECTS

FIG. 18. Ceremonial sticks.

Among various wooden objects found at Spruce-tree House may be mentioned sticks resembling prayer offerings and others which may have been employed in ceremonials (fig. 18.)

A fragment of a primitive fire-stick (fig. 19) was obtained from the northern refuse-heap and near it were straight sticks that undoubtedly served as fire-drills. There were one or two needles (fig. 20), made of hard wood, suggesting weaving or some similar process. A fragment of an arrow was unearthed in the débris of the northern refuse-heap.

FIG. 19. Primitive fire-stick.

FIG. 20. Wooden needle.

FABRICS

The yucca plant, which grows wild in the canyons and level places of the Mesa Verde, furnishes a tough fiber which the prehistoric people of Spruce-tree House used in the manufacture of various

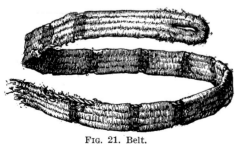

FIG. 21. Belt.

fabrics. Small packages of this fiber and cords made of the same material were found in the refuse-heap and in the houses; these were apparently obtained by heating and chewing the leaves, after which the fiber was drawn out into cords or braided into strings.

A braided cord was also found attached to the handles of jars, and this fiber was a favorite one in mending pottery. It was almost universally employed in weaving cloth netting and other fabrics, where it was combined with cotton fiber. Belts (fig. 21) or head-bands (figs. 22, 23) show the best examples of this weaving. Native cotton fiber is not as common as yucca, being more difficult apparently to procure. There is some doubt regarding the cultivation of the

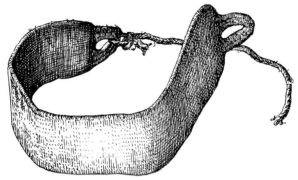

FIG. 22. Headband.

cotton plant, and no cotton seeds were identified; the cloth woven from this fiber shows great skill in weaving.

The bark of willows and alders was utilized for fabrics, but this furnished material for basketry rather than for cloth.

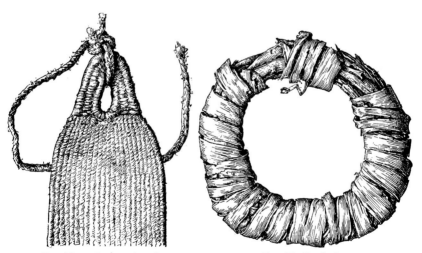

FIG. 23. End of headband.   FIG. 24. Head ring.

One of the most beautiful specimens of woven cloth yet obtained in the Mesa Verde ruins was taken from room 11; this is apparently a headband for carrying bundles.

Among the objects obtained in the northern refuse heap were rings made of the leaf and fiber of yucca and other plants, sometimes blackened as if by fire (fig. 24). These rings may have been used for carrying jars on the head, although some are too large and flat for that purpose. It has been suggested that the largest were used in some game, but this theory lacks confirmation.

Small fragments of matting were found, but no complete specimen came to light. These fragments resemble those referred to by Nordenskiöld as "objects used in carpeting the floors." It was customary

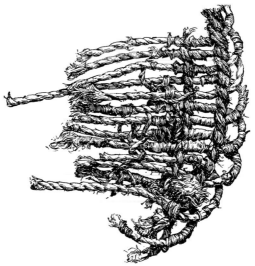

FIG. 25. Yucca-fiber cloth with attached feathers.

among some of the sedentary Indians of the Southwest to sleep on rectangular mats, and in one building of compound B of Casa Grande impressions of these mats were found on the floor.

Fragments of cloth made of yucca fiber (fig. 25), in which feathers are woven, are abundant in the refuse heaps of Spruce-tree House.

FIG. 26. Woven cord.

There were found also many strings in which feathers were woven (fig. 26), but of these nothing but the midribs remain.

The object shown in figure 27 is made of agave fiber tied in a series of loops. Its use is unknown.

Several sandals were excavated at Spruce-tree House, the majority from the refuse-heap in the rear of the dwellings. One of these specimens, figure 28, is in good condition; it is evidently a mortuary object, being found near a skeleton. The other specimen (fig. 29) is fragmentary, consisting of a sole of a sandal with attached toe cords.

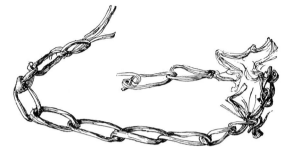

FIG. 27. Agave fiber tied in loops.

FIG. 28. Woven moccasin.

FIG. 29. Fragment of sandal.

FIG. 30. Hair-brush.

Several specimens of slender yucca leaves bound in a bundle were found. One of these (fig. 30) served as a hair-brush, or was used in stirring food. One brush made of finer material was collected.

BONE IMPLEMENTS

A large collection of beautiful bone implements (see fig. 31)—
needles, awls, tubes, and dirks—rewarded the work at Spruce-tree

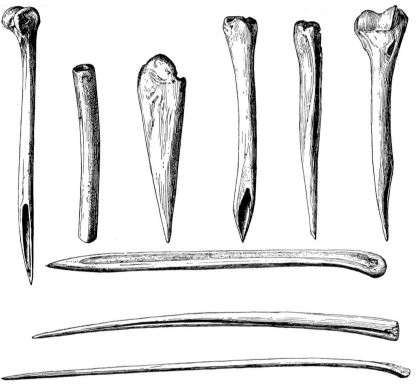

Fig. 31. Bone implements.

House. Some of these show the effects of fire throughout their
length, while others are smoked only at one end. When unearthed,

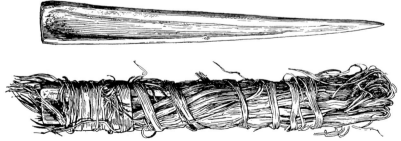

Fig. 32. Dirk and cedar-bark sheath.

one of these dirks was still in the original sheath of cedar bark
(fig. 32).

Most of the needles, bodkins, and awls are made of bones of birds or small animals. These were apparently rubbed down and pointed

FIG. 33. Bone implement.

on stone implements or on the sides of the cliff, where grooves are often found (fig. 33).

FIG. 34. Bone scraper.

Several fine bone scrapers (figs. 34, 35) were dug out of the débris covering the floors of the rooms. These are beveled to a sharp edge at one end, the trochanter of the bone serving as a handle.

FIG. 35. Bone scraper.

FETISH

Only one fetish in the form of a human being was obtained at Spruce-tree House, this being found in the débris near the floor of kiva G. So far as the objects from Mesa Verde ruins have been figured or described, this is the first record of the finding of a fetish of human shape in any of these ruins. Moreover, such a fetish is a rarity in cliff-house ruins elsewhere in the Southwest, a fact which imparts to this specimen more than usual interest.

LIGNITE GORGET

In the author's account of his excavations in ruins in the Little Colorado valley there was figured a large fragment of a disk made of cannel coal or lignite. This disk is convex on one side and plain on the side opposite, the latter having an eyelet, or two holes for suspension. A lignite gorget, similar for the most part to the above-mentioned specimen, but differing therefrom in having the eyelet in the convex instead of in the flat side, was found at Spruce-tree House. Probably both objects were formerly used as ornaments, being suspended about the neck. No similar specimen has thus far been described from Mesa Verde ruins.

CORN, BEANS, AND SQUASH SEEDS

All indications point to maize, or Indian corn, as the chief food plant of the prehistoric people of this cliff-dwelling. This is ,evident not only from the presence in the ruins of metates and grinding stones, but also from the abundance of corn ears and other fragments discovered; corn husks and seed corn were especially plentiful in rooms and in the refuse-heaps. As in the case of the modern Pueblos, the corn appears to have been of several colors, while the size of the cobs indicates that the ears were small with but few rows of seeds. In addition to cobs, fragments of corn stalks, leaves, and even tassels were found in some of the rooms. Beans of the brown variety, specimens of which were numerous in one room, were the most esteemed. There were obtained also stalks and portions of gourds some of which are artificially perforated, as well as a gourd the rind of which is almost complete. Apparently these gourds were used for ceremonial rattles and for drinking vessels. The form suggests that of a Hopi netted gourd in which sacred water is brought from distant springs for use in the kivas, or ceremonial rooms.

HOOP-AND-POLE GAME

It appears from the discovery of a small wooden hoop in one of the rooms that the prehistoric people of Spruce-tree House were

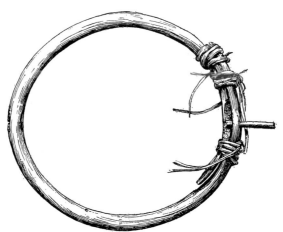

FIG. 36. Hoop used in hoop-and-pole game.

familiar with the hoop-and-pole game (fig. 36) so popular among several of our aboriginal tribes. But whether or not the individual hoop obtained was used in a secular game or a ceremony may be open to differences of opinion. The author is inclined to connect the specimen above referred to with basket dances, one of which is called by the Hopi the *Owakulti.*[a] In this dance the hoop is rolled on the ground and the players throw or attempt to throw darts through it.

LEATHER AND SKIN OBJECTS

Fragments of leather or dressed skin (fig. 37) were found in several of the rooms. These are apparently parts of moccasins or sandals, but may have been pouches or similar objects. A strip of rawhide by means of which an ax was lashed to its handle was picked

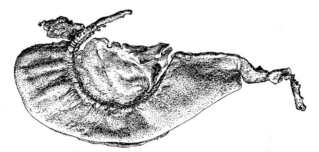

FIG. 37. Portion of leather moccasin.

up in the dump, where also was a fragment of what may have been a leather pouch with a thong of hide woven in one edge. If skins of animals were used for clothing, as they probably were, but slight evidence of the fact remains.

ABSENCE OF OBJECTS SHOWING EUROPEAN CULTURE

In the excavations which were necessary to clean out the rooms of Spruce-tree House no object of European make was discovered. There was no sign of any metal, even copper being unrepresented; no object discovered shows traces of cutting by knives or other implements made of metal. Evidently European culture exerted no influence on the aborigines of Spruce-tree House.

PICTOGRAPHS

Near Spruce-tree House, as elsewhere on the Mesa Verde, are found examples of those rock-etchings and other markings known as pictographs. Some of these represent human beings in various attitudes, and animals, as deer, mountain sheep, snakes, and other subjects not

---

[a] See figure of Owakulti altar in the author's account of the Owakulti. Mr. Stewart Culin thus comments on the " hoop-and-pole " game among Pueblos : " Similar ceremonies or games were practised by the cliff-dwellers, as is attested by a number of objects from Mancos canyon, Colorado, in the Free Museum of Science and Art of the University of Pennsylvania."—*Twenty-fourth Annual Report of the Bureau of American Ethnology.*

yet determined. As seems to be true of the other rock-inscriptions just mentioned, some of those near Spruce-tree House are religious symbols, some are totems, while others are mere scribblings.

These pictographs are so rude that they give little idea of the artistic possibilities of their makers, while many are so worn that even the subjects intended to be depicted are doubtful.

The walls of some of the rooms in the Mesa Verde cliff-dwellings still show figures painted while the rooms were inhabited. Among these the favorite designs are of triangular form.

The walls of the secular rooms and kivas of Spruce-tree House were formerly covered with a thin wash of colored sand which was well adapted for paintings of symbolic or decorative character. The colors (yellow, red, and white), were evidently put on with the hands, impressions of which can be found in several places. In some cases, as with the upper part of the wall painted white and the lower part red, the contrast brings out the colors very effectively. The walls of some of the rooms are blackened with smoke.

Among the designs used are the triangular figures on the upper margin of the dados and pedestals of kivas. Figures similar in form, but reversed, are made by the Hopi, who call them butterfly and raincloud symbols.

Birds and quadrupeds.—Nordenskiöld (pp. 108–9) thus writes of one of the ancient paintings:

> The first of them, fig. 77, is executed in a room at Sprucetree House. Here too the lower part of the mural surface is dark red, and triangular points of the same colour project over the yellow plaster; above this lower part of the wall runs a row of red dots, exactly as in the estufa at Ruin 9. To the left two figures are painted, one of them evidently representing a bird, the other a quadruped with large horns, probably a mountain sheep. [Elsewhere, as quoted on p. 5. Nordenskiöld identifies these figures as "two birds."] The painting shown in fig. 78 is similar in style to the two just described.

In this room the dado bears at intervals along its upper edge the triangular figures already noticed, and rows of dots which appear to be a symbolic decoration, occurring likewise on pottery, as an examination of the author's collection makes evident.

Square figures.—On the eastern wall of the same room in which occur the figures of a bird and a horned mammal there is a square figure on the white surface of the upper wall. This figure is black in outline; part of the surface bears an angular meander similar to decorations on some pieces of pottery. Similar designs, arranged in series according to Mindeleff's figures, form the decoration band of one of the kivas in Chelly canyon.

The significance of this figure is unknown but its widespread distribution, especially in that region of the Southwest characterized by circular kivas, adds considerable interest to its interpretation.

Terraced figure.—Covering almost the whole side of a wall north of kiva C and overlooking the plaza of which this room forms in part the northern wall, is a conspicuous figure painted white. If we regard the building of which this is a side as formerly two stories high, this painting would have been on the inside of a room, otherwise we have the exceptional feature of a painting on an outer wall. The purpose of this painting is not clear to the author, but similar figures, reversed, signify rain clouds. The figure recalls in form a representation of a T-shaped doorway and appears to be a unique one among Mesa Verde ruins.

CONCLUSIONS

From the preceding facts it is evident that the people who once inhabited Spruce-tree House were not highly developed in culture, although the buildings show an advanced order of architecture for aborigines of North America. Architecturally the cliff-dwellings excel pueblos of more recent construction.

The pottery is not inferior to that of other parts of the Southwest, but has fewer symbols and is not as fine or varied in colors as that from Sikyatki or from Casas Grandes in Sonora. It is better than the pottery from the Casa Grande and other compounds of the Gila and about the same in texture and symbols as that from Chelly canyon and Chaco canyon.

The remaining minor antiquities, as cloth, basketry, wood, and bone, are of the same general character as those found elsewhere in the Southwest. Shell work is practically lacking; no objects made from marine shells have been found.

The picture of culture drawn from what we know of the life at Spruce-tree House is practically the same as that of a pueblo like Walpi at the time of its discovery by whites, and until about fifty years ago. The people were farmers, timid, industrious, and superstitious. The women were skillful potters and made fine baskets. The men made cloth of good quality and cultivated corn, beans, and melons.

In the long winters the kivas served as the lounging places for the men who were engaged in an almost constant round of ceremonies of dramatic character, which took the place of the pleasures of the chase. They never ventured far from home and rarely met strangers. They had all those unsocial characteristics which an isolated life fosters.

What language they spoke, and whether various Mesa Verde Houses had the same language, at present no one can tell. The culture was selfcentered and apparently well developed. It is not known whether it originated in the Mesa Verde canyons or was completely evolved when it reached there.

Although we know little about the culture of the prehistoric inhabitants of Mesa Verde, it does not follow that we can not find out more. There are many ruins awaiting exploration in this region and future work will reveal much which has been so long hidden.

The pressure of outside tribes, or what may be called human environment, probably had much to do originally with the choice of caves for houses, and the magnificent caverns of the Mesa Verde naturally attracted men as favorable sites for their houses. The habit of huddling together in a limited space, necessitated by a life in the cliffs, possibly developed the composite form which still persists in the pueblo form of architecture.

INDEX

O

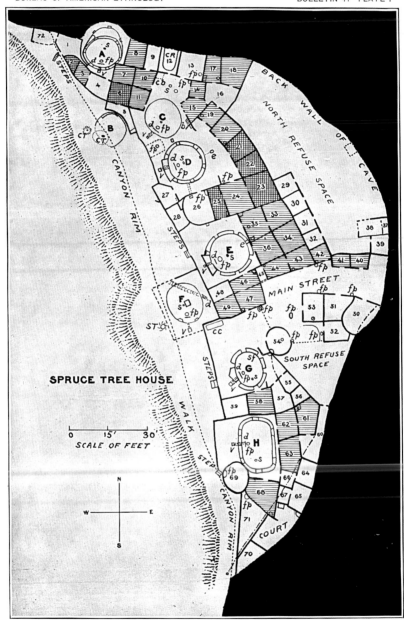

GROUND PLAN OF SPRUCE-TREE HOUSE

From the northwest

From the west

THE RUIN, FROM THE NORTHWEST AND THE WEST

Before repairing

After repairing

PLAZA D

Before repairing

After repairing

THE RUIN, FROM THE SOUTH END

THE RUIN, FROM THE SOUTH

General view

Room 11, from the south

ROOMS 11-24

THE RUIN, FROM THE NORTH END

NORTH END OF THE RUIN, SHOWING MASONRY PILLAR

Roof of room 43

Main street

A ROOF AND A STREET

Front of rooms 62 and 63

Plaza E, from the south, before repair

THE RUIN FROM THE SOUTH END, SHOWING ROOMS AND PLAZA

Before repairing

After repairing

KIVA D

KIVA D, FROM THE NORTH

Kiva A, repaired

Kiva D, repaired

INTERIORS OF TWO KIVAS

From stump of spruce tree, looking east

Interior of kiva C, looking southwest

CENTRAL PART OF RUIN, AND KIVA

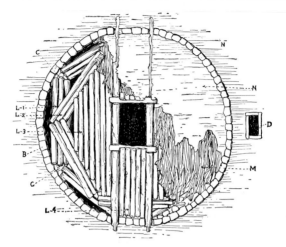

From above, showing roof

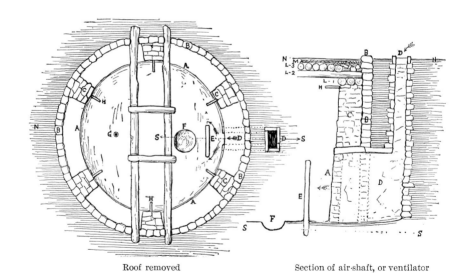

Roof removed   Section of air-shaft, or ventilator

DIAGRAMS OF KIVA, SHOWING CONSTRUCTION

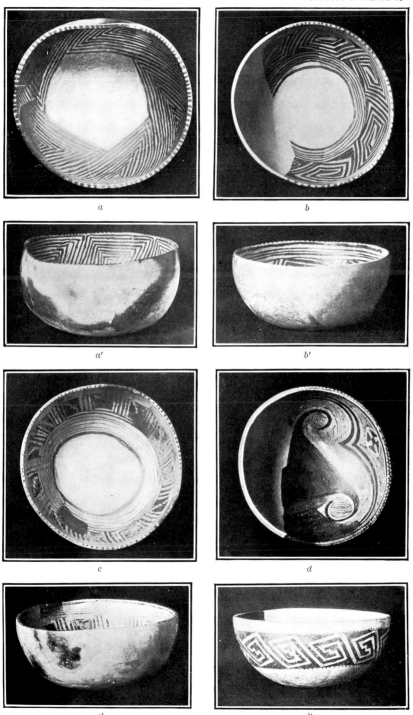

a   b

a′   b′

c   d

c′   d′

DECORATED FOOD-BOWLS

Diameters (in inches): a, $a′$, $11\frac{1}{4}$; b, $b′$, 11; c, $c′$, $11\frac{1}{2}$; d, $d′$, $9\frac{1}{8}$

DECORATED FOOD-BOWLS

Diameters (in inches): a, a′, 11; b, b′, 13; c, c′, 11½

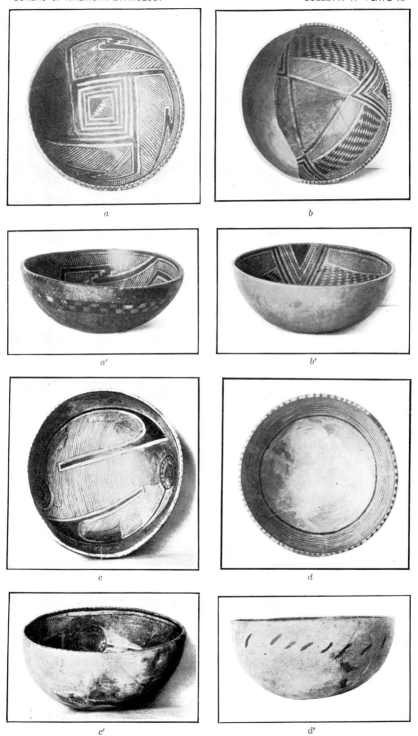

DECORATED FOOD-BOWLS

Diameters (in inches): *a, a′*, 9; *b, b′*, 12¼; *c, c′*, 11; *d, d′*, 11¾

a

b

c

d

e

f

DECORATED VASE AND MUGS

Heights (in inches): *a*, 3⅓; *b*, 3⅜; *c*, 3⅝; *d*, 4¼; *e*, 3¾; *f*, 5

a. Small bowl (diam., 3¾ in.)

b. Two-handled globular canteen (height, 7¼ in.)

DECORATED BOWL AND CANTEEN

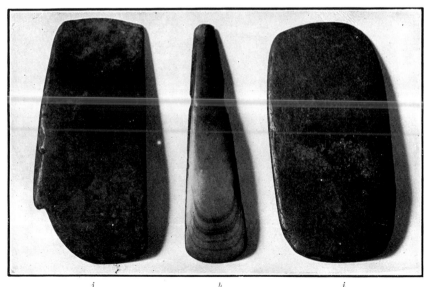

STONE IMPLEMENTS

a–g, axes; *h*, tcamahia; *i*, paint stone; *j*, paint stone (last?)

Lengths (in inches): *a*, 4¼; *b*, 4¾; *c*, 5; *d*, 5¼; *e*, 6¼; *f*, 6⅞; *g*, 5¾; *h*, 10½; *i*, 10¼; *j*, 10¾

SMITHSONIAN INSTITUTION
BUREAU OF AMERICAN ETHNOLOGY
BULLETIN 51

ANTIQUITIES OF THE MESA VERDE NATIONAL PARK

CLIFF PALACE

BY

JESSE WALTER FEWKES

WASHINGTON
GOVERNMENT PRINTING OFFICE
1911

LETTER OF TRANSMITTAL

SMITHSONIAN INSTITUTION,
BUREAU OF AMERICAN ETHNOLOGY,
Washington, D. C., May 14, 1910.

SIR: I have the honor to submit the accompanying manuscript, entitled "Antiquities of the Mesa Verde National Park: Cliff Palace," by Dr. Jesse Walter Fewkes, with the recommendation that it be published, subject to your approval, as Bulletin 51 of this Bureau.

Yours, very respectfully,

F. W. HODGE,
Ethnologist in Charge.

Dr. CHARLES D. WALCOTT,
Secretary of the Smithsonian Institution,
Washington, D. C.

3

CONTENTS

ILLUSTRATIONS

ANTIQUITIES OF THE MESA VERDE NATIONAL PARK

CLIFF PALACE

By Jesse Walter Fewkes

INTRODUCTION

In the summer of 1909 the writer was detailed by the Secretary of the Smithsonian Institution, at the request of the Secretary of the Interior, to continue the excavation and repair of ruins in the Mesa Verde National Park, Colorado. This work was placed under his sole charge and continued through the months May to August, inclusive. In that time the writer was able to repair completely this great ruin and to leave it in such condition that tourists and students visiting it may learn much more about cliff-dwellings than was possible before the work was undertaken.

The force of laborers, numbering on an average 15 workmen, was from Mancos, Colorado. Many of them had worked on Spruce-tree House during the previous year and had become expert in repairing ruins. By their aid it was possible to accomplish more and at less expense than was expected. It has fallen to the writer to prepare the report on the work which he had the honor to direct, and he is conscious how difficult it is to put it into a form that will adequately express the devotion with which those under him have accomplished their respective tasks.

A report on the general results accomplished at Cliff Palace was published by the Secretary of the Interior in 1909; the following account considers in a more detailed way the various scientific phases. The purpose of the present paper is to present a more accurate account of Cliff Palace than was possible before the excavation and repair work was done, and to increase existing knowledge by directing attention to the scientific data revealed by excavations of this largest, most picturesque, and most typical cliff-dwelling in the Southwest. In order to give this account a monographic form there have been introduced the most important descriptions of Cliff Palace previously published. There is also included a description of the few minor antiquities brought to light in the progress of the work. These specimens are now in the United States National Museum, where they form the nucleus of a collection from Cliff Palace. The increasing interest, local and national, in the prehistoric culture of the Southwest and the influence of these antiquities in attracting visitors to localities where they exist, furnish a reason for considering in some detail various other questions of general interest connected with cliff-dwellings that naturally suggest themselves to those interested in the history of man in America.

The method of work in this undertaking has been outlined in the report on Spruce-tree House published by the Secretary of the Interior.[a] The primary thought has been to increase the educational value of Cliff Palace by attracting tourists and students of archeology.

The reader is reminded that from the nature of the work at Cliff Palace very few specimens can be expected from it in the future, and that so far as the minor antiquities are concerned the objective material from this ruin is now all deposited in public museums or in private collections. Additional specimens can be obtained, however, from other ruins near it which will throw light on the culture of Cliff Palace. It is appropriate, therefore, to point out, at the very threshold of our consideration, that a continuation of archeological work in the Mesa Verde National Park is desirable, as it will add to our knowledge of the character of prehistoric life in these canyons. The next work to be undertaken should be the excavation and repair of a Mesa Verde pueblo. The extensive mounds of stone and earth on the promontory west of Cliff Palace have not yet been excavated, and offer attractive possibilities for study and a promise of many specimens. Buried in these mounds there are undoubtedly many rooms, secular and ceremonial, which a season's work could uncover, thus enlarging indirectly our knowledge of the cliff-dwellers and their descendants.[b]

The writer considers it an honor to have been placed in charge of the excavation and repair of Cliff Palace, and takes this occasion to express high appreciation of his indebtedness to both the Secretary of the Smithsonian Institution and the Secretary of the Interior for their confidence in his judgment in this difficult undertaking.

Maj. Hans M. Randolph, superintendent of the Mesa Verde National Park, gave assistance in purchasing the equipment, making out accounts, and in other ways. During the sojourn at Cliff Palace the writer was accompanied by Mr. R. G. Fuller, of the Peabody Museum of Harvard University, a volunteer assistant, who con-

---

[a] In his Annual Report for 1908. See also *Bulletin 41 of the Bureau of American Ethnology.*

[b] A few holes that have been dug here and there in these mounds have brought to light sections of walls with good masonry, but no excavations that could be called extensive or scientific have yet been attempted on this site. The excavation of these mounds might reveal a pueblo like Walpi, and a comparison of objects from them with those from Cliff Palace would be important in tracing the relationship of cliff-dwellings and pueblos.

tributed some of the photographs used in the preparation of the plates that accompany this report. The writer is indebted also to Mr. F. K. Vreeland, of Montclair, New Jersey, for several fine photographs of Cliff Palace taken before the repairing was done.

CLIFF PALACE A TYPE OF PREHISTORIC CULTURE

In the following pages the walls and other remains of buildings and the objects found in the rooms have been treated from their cultural point of view. Considering ethnology, or culture history, as the comparative study of mental productions of groups of men in different epochs, and cultural archeology as a study of those objects belonging to a time antedating recorded history, there has been sought in Cliff Palace one type of prehistoric American culture, or rather a type of the mental production of a group of men in an environment where, so far as external influences are concerned, caves, mesas, and cliffs are predominant and aridity is a dominant climatic factor. Primarily archeology is a study of the expression of human intelligence, and it must be continually borne in mind that Cliff Palace was once the home of men and women whose minds responded to their surroundings. It is hoped that this monograph will be a contribution to a study of the influence of environment on the material condition of a group of prehistoric people. The condition of culture here brought to light is in part a result of experiences transmitted from one generation to another, but while this heritage of culture is due to environment, intensified by each transmission, there are likewise in it survivals of the culture due to antecedent environments, which have also been preserved by heredity, but has diminished in proportion, pari passu, as the epoch in which they originated is farther and farther removed in time from the environment that created them. These survivals occur mostly in myths and religious cult objects, and are the last to be abandoned when man changes his environment.

It is believed that one advantage of a series of monographic descriptions of these ruins is found in the fact that the characteristics of individual ruins being known, more accurate generalizations concerning the entire culture will later be made possible by comparative studies. There is an individuality in Cliff Palace, not only in its architecture but also in a still greater measure in the symbolism of the pottery decoration. These features vary more or less in different ruins, notwithstanding their former inhabitants were of similar culture. These variations are lost in a general description of that culture.

The reader is asked to bear in mind that when the repair of Cliff Palace was undertaken the vandalism wrought by those who had dug into it had destroyed much data and greatly reduced the possibility of generalizations on the character of its culture. The ruin had been almost completely rifled of its contents, the specimens removed, and its walls left in a very dilapidated condition. Much of the excavation carried on under the writer's supervision yielded meager scientific results so far as the discovery of specimens was concerned; throughout the summer earth was being dug over that had already been examined and cult objects removed. Had it been possible to have begun work on Cliff Palace just after the ruin was deserted by the aboriginal inhabitants, or, as that was impossible, at least anticipated only by the destruction wrought by the elements, these explorations might have illumined many difficult problems which must forever remain unsolved.

The present monograph is the second in a series dealing with the antiquities of the Mesa Verde National Park and opening with the account of the excavation and repair of Spruce-tree House.[a] An exhaustive account of all known antiquities from Cliff Palace is not intended, and no reference is made even to many objects from that ruin now in museums. Discussion of details is not so much aimed at as brevity in the statement of results and a contribution to our knowledge of a typical form of Southwestern culture. Believing that modern Pueblo culture is the direct descendant of that of cliff-dwellers, the writer has not hesitated to make use of ethnology, when possible, in an interpretation of the archeological material.

Although the name Cliff Palace is not altogether an appropriate one for this ruin, it is now too firmly fixed in the literature of cliff-dwellings to be changed. The term " palace " implies a higher social development than that which existed in this village, which undoubtedly had a house chief similar to the village chief (*kimongwi*) of the Hopi, who occupied that position on account of being the oldest man of the oldest clan; but this ruin is not the remains of a " palace " of such a chief.

The population of Cliff Palace was composed of many clans, more or less distinct and independent, which were rapidly being amalgamated by marriage; so we may regard the population as progressing toward a homogeneous community. Cliff Palace was practically a pueblo built in a cave; its population grew from both without and within: new clans from time to time joined those existing, while new births continually augmented the number of inhabitants.

There was no water at Cliff Palace [b] when work began, but a good supply was developed in the canyon below the ruin, where there is every reason to believe the former inhabitants had their well. In a neighboring canyon, separated from that in which Cliff Palace is

---

[a] *Bulletin 41 of the Bureau of American Ethnology.*

[b] All potable water for camp had to be brought from Spruce-tree House, about 2 miles away.

situated by a promontory at the north, there is also a meager seepage
of water which was developed incidentally into a considerable supply.
In the cliff above this water is a large cave in which was discovered
the walls of a kiva of the second type, but the falling of a large block
of rock upon it—which occurred subsequent to the construction of
this kiva—led to its abandonment. This cave is extensive enough
for a cliff-house as large as Cliff Palace; but for this accident it
might have developed into a formidable rival of the latter.

RECENT HISTORY

It is remarkable that this magnificent ruin (pl. 1) so long escaped
knowledge of white settlers in the neighboring Montezuma valley.
Cliff Palace is not mentioned in early Spanish writings, and, indeed,
the first description of it was not published until about 1890.

Efforts to learn the name of the white man who discovered Cliff
Palace were not rewarded with great success. According to Nordenskiöld it was first seen by Richard Wetherill and Charley Mason
on a " December day in 1888," but several residents of the towns of
Mancos and Cortez claim to have visited it before that time. One of
the first of these visitors was a cattle owner of Mancos, Mr. James
Frink, who told the author that he first saw Cliff Palace in 1881, and
as several stockmen were with him at that time it is probable that
there are others who visited it the same year. We may conclude that
Cliff Palace was unknown to scientific men in 1880, and the most we
can definitely say is that it was first seen by white men some time in
the decade 1880–1890.[a]

While there is considerable literature on the cliff-dwellings of the
Mesa Verde, individual ruins have not been exhaustively described.
Much less has been published on Spruce-tree House than on Cliff
Palace, which latter ruin, being the largest, has attracted more attention than any other in the Park. As every cliff-house has its peculiar
architectural features it is well in describing these buildings to refer
to the ruins by names. This individuality in architecture pertains
likewise to specimens, the majority of which in museums unfortunately are labeled merely " Mancos " or " Mesa Verde." A large
number of these objects probably came from Spruce-tree House and
Cliff Palace, but it is now impossible to determine their exact
derivation.

The first extended account of Cliff Palace, accompanied with illustrations, which is worthy of special mention, was published by Mr.
F. H. Chapin, and so far as priority of publication is concerned he

---

[a] It is generally stated by stockmen and others who claim to have seen Cliff Palace
" years ago," that the walls of the buildings were much higher in the early eighties than
they are at present.

may be regarded as the first to make Cliff Palace known to the scientific world. Almost simultaneously with his article there appeared an account of the ruin by Doctor Birdsall, followed shortly by the superbly illustrated memoir of Baron Gustav Nordenskiöld. All these writers adopt the name Cliff Palace, which apparently was first given to the ruin by Richard Wetherill, one of the claimants for its discovery. Nordenskiöld's work contains practically all that was known about Cliff Palace up to the beginning of the summer's field work herein described.

Mr. Chapin [a] thus referred to Cliff Palace in a paper read before The Appalachian Mountain Club on February 13, 1890:

After a long ride we reached a camping-ground at the head of a branch of the left-hand fork of Cliff Cañon. Hurriedly unpacking, we hobbled the horses that were the most likely to stray far, and taking along our photographic kit, wended our way on foot toward that remarkable group of ruins of which I have already spoken, and which Richard has called "the Cliff-Palace." At about three o'clock we reached the brink of the cañon opposite the wonderful structure. Surely its discoverer had not overstated the beauty and magnitude of this strange ruin. There it was, occupying a great oval space under a grand cliff wonderful to behold, appearing like an immense ruined castle with dismantled towers. The stones in front were broken away, but behind them rose the walls of a second story; and in the rear of these, in under the dark cavern, stood the third tier of masonry. Still farther back in the gloomy recess, little houses rested on upper ledges. A short distance down the cañon are cosey buildings perched in utterly inaccessible nooks. The neighboring scenery is marvelous; the view down the cañon to the Mancos is alone worth the journey to see. We stopped to take a few views, and then commenced the descent into the gulf below. What would otherwise have been a hazardous proceeding, was rendered easy by using the steps which had been cut in the wall by the builders of the fortress. There are fifteen of these scouped-out hollows in the rock, which covered perhaps half of the distance down the precipice. At that point the cliff had probably fallen away; but luckily for our purpose, a dead tree leaned against the wall, and descending into its branches we reached the base of the parapet. In the bed of the cañon is a secondary gulch, which required care in descending. We hung a rope or lasso over some steep, smooth ledges, and let ourselves down by it. We left it hanging there and used it to ascend by on our return.

Nearer approach increased our interest in the marvel. From the south end of the ruin, which we first attained, trees hide the northern walls, yet the view is beautiful. We remained long, and ransacked the structure from one end to the other. According to Richard's measurements, the space covered by the building is 425 feet long, 80 feet high in front, and 80 feet deep in the centre. One hundred and twenty-four rooms have been traced on the ground floor, and a thousand people may have lived within its confines. So many walls have fallen that it is difficult to reconstruct the building in imagination; but the photographs show that there must have been many stories. There are towers and circular rooms, square and rectangular enclosures; yet all with a seeming symmetry, though in some places the walls look as if they were put up as additions in later periods. One of the towers is barrel-shaped; other circles are true.

---

[a] *Appalachia*, VI, 28–30, May, 1890, Boston, 1892.

The diameter of one circular room, or estufa, is sixteen feet and six inches. There are six piers, which are well plastered. There are five recess-holes, which appear as if constructed for shelves. In several rooms we observed good fire-places. In another room, where the outer walls have fallen away, we found that an attempt had been made at ornamentation: a broad band had been painted across the wall, and above it is a peculiar decoration which shows in one of our photographs. The lines are similar to embellishment on pottery which we found. We observed in one place corn-cobs imbedded in the plaster in the walls, showing that the cob is as old as that portion of the dwelling. The cobs, as well as kernels of corn which we found, are of small size, similar to what the Ute squaws raise now without irrigation. We found a large stone mortar, which may have been used to grind the corn. Broken pottery was everywhere; like specimens in the other cliff houses, it was similar in design to that which we picked up in the valley ruins near Wetherill's ranch, convincing us of the identity of the builders of the two classes of ruins. We also found parts of skulls and bones, fragments of weapons, and pieces of cloth. One nearly complete skeleton lies on a wall waiting for some future antiquarian. The burial-place of the clan was down under the rear of the cave.

Dr. W. R. Birdsall,[a] who in 1891 gave an account of the cliff-dwellings of the canyons of the Mesa Verde, which contains considerable information regarding these buildings, thus refers specially to Cliff Palace:

Richard Wetherill discovered an unusually large group of buildings which he named "The Cliff Palace," in which the ground plan showed more than one hundred compartments, covering an area over four hundred feet in length and eighty feet in depth in the wider portion. Usually the buildings are continuous where the configuration of the cliffs permitted such construction.

In the following account Baron Nordenskiöld has given us the most exhaustive description of Cliff Palace yet published:[b]

In a long, but not very deep branch of Cliff Cañon, a wild and gloomy gorge named Cliff Palace Cañon, lies the largest of the ruins on the Mesa Verde, the Cliff Palace. Strange and indescribable is the impression on the traveller, when, after a long and tiring ride through the boundless, monotonous piñon forest, he suddenly halts on the brink of the precipice, and in the opposite cliff beholds the ruins of the Cliff Palace, framed in the massive vault of rock above and in a bed of sunlit cedar and piñon trees below (Pl. XII). This ruin well deserves its name, for with its round towers and high walls rising out of the heaps of stones deep in the mysterious twilight of the cavern, and defying in their sheltered site the ravages of time, it resembles at a distance an enchanted castle. It is not surprising that the Cliff Palace so long remained undiscovered. An attempt to follow Cliff Palace Cañon upward from Cliff Cañon meets with almost insurmountable obstacles in the shape of huge blocks of stone which have fallen from the cliffs and formed a barrier across the narrow water course, in most parts of the cañon the only practicable path between the steep walls of rock. Through the piñon forest, which renders the mesa a perfect labyrinth to

---

[a] *Jour. Amer. Geog. Soc.*, XXIII, no. 4, 598, New York, 1891.

[b] In The Cliff Dwellers of the Mesa Verde (a translation in English from the Swedish edition, Stockholm, 1893), (pp. 59–66), unfortunately not accessible to most readers on account of the limited edition and the cost. For this reason the description is here reproduced in extenso. (The references to illustrations and the footnotes in this excerpt follow Nordenskiöld.)

the uninitiated, chance alone can guide the explorer to the exact spot from which a view of Cliff Palace is possible.

The descent to the ruin may be made from the mesa either on the opposite side of the cañon, or on the same a few hundred paces north or south of the cliff-dwelling. The Cliff Palace is probably the largest ruin of its kind known in the United States. I here give a plan of the ruin (Pl. XI) together with a photograph thereof, taken from the south end of the cave (Pl. XII). In the plan, which represents the ground floor, over a hundred rooms are shown. About twenty of them are estufas. Among the rubbish and stones in front of the ruin a few more walls, not marked in the plan. may possibly be distinguished.

Plate XIII, as I have just mentioned, is a photograph of the Cliff Palace from the south. To the extreme left of the plate a number of much dilapidated walls may be seen. They correspond to rooms 1–12 in the plan. To the right of these walls lies a whole block of rooms (13–18), several stories high and built on a huge rock which has fallen from the roof of the cave. The outermost room (14 in the plan; to the left in Pl. XIII) is bounded on the outside by a high wall, the outlines of which stand off sharply from the dark background of the cave. The wall is built in a quadrant at the edge of the rock just mentioned, which has been carefully dressed, the wall thus forming apparently an immediate continuation of the rock. The latter is coursed by a fissure which also extends through the wall. This crevice must therefore have appeared subsequent to the building operation. To the right of this curved wall (still in Pl. XIII) lie four rooms (15–18 in the plan), and in front of them two terraces (21–22) connected by a step. One of the rooms is surrounded by walls three stories high and reaching up to the roof of the cave. The terraces are bounded to the north (the left in Pl. XIII) by a rather high wall, standing apart from the remainder of the building. Not far from the rooms just mentioned, but a little farther back, lie two cylindrical chambers (21 a, 23). The wall of 21 a is shown in Pl. XIII with a beam resting against it. The beam had been placed there by one of the Wetherills to assist him in climbing to an upper ledge, where low walls, resembling the fortress at Long House (p. 28), rise almost to the roof of the cave. The round room 23 is joined by a wall to a long series of chambers (26–41), which are very low, though their walls extend to the rock above them. They probably served as storerooms. These chambers front on a "street," on the opposite side of which lie a number of apartments[a] (42–50), among them a remarkable estufa (44) described at greater length below. In front of 44 lies another estufa (51), and not far from the latter a third (52).

The "street" leads to an open space. Here lie three estufas (54, 55, 56), partly sunk in the ground. Much lower down is situated another estufa (57) of the same type as 44. It is surrounded by high walls.[b] South of the open space lie a few large rooms (58–61). A tower (63 in the plan; the large tower to the right in Pl. XIII) is situated still farther south, beside a steep ledge. This ledge, north of the tower (to the left in the plate), once formed a free terrace (62), bounded on the outside by a low wall along the margin. South of the tower is an estufa (76) surrounded by an open space, southeast of which are a number of rooms (80–87). In most of them, even in the outermost ones, the walls are in an excellent state of preservation. The wall

---

[a] The room marked 48 in the plan is visible in Pl. XIII. Almost in the center of the plate, but a little to the right, two small loopholes may be seen, and to their right a doorway, all of which belong to room 48; the walls of 49 and 50 are much lower than those of 48. Behind 48 the high walls of 43 may be distinguished.

[b] They are shown in the plate just to the left of the fold at its middle, rather low down.

nearest to the talus slope is 6 metres high and built with great care and skill.[a] South of these rooms and close to the cliff lies a well-preserved estufa (88), and south of the latter four rooms are situated, two of them (90, 92) very small. The walls of the third (91) are very high and rise to the roof of the cave. At one corner the walls have fallen in. This room is figured in a subsequent chapter in order to show a painting found on one of its walls. Near the cliff lies the last estufa (93), in an excellent state of preservation. The rooms south of this estufa are bounded on the outer side by a high wall rising to the rock above it. An excellent defense was thus provided against attack in this quarter.

Two of the estufas in the Cliff Palace deviate from the normal type. This is the only instance where I have observed estufas differing in construction from the ordinary form described in Chapter III. The northern estufa (44 in the plan) is the better preserved of the two. To a height of 1 meter from the floor it is square in form (3×3 m.) with rounded corners (see figs. 35 and 36). Above it is wider and bounded by the walls of the surrounding rooms, a ledge (b, b) of irregular shape being thus formed a few feet from the floor. In two of the rounded corners on a level with this ledge (a little to the right in fig. 36) niches or hollows (d, d; breadth 48 cm., depth 45 cm.) have been constructed, and between them, at the middle of the south-east wall, a narrow passage (breadth 40 cm.), open at the top. At the bottom of one side of this passage a continuation thereof was found, corresponding probably to the tunnel in estufas of the ordinary type. At the north corner of the room the wall is broken by three small niches (e, e, e) quite close together, each of them occupying a space about equal to that left by the removal of two stones from the wall. The sandstone blocks of which the walls are built are carefully hewn, as in the ordinary cylindrical estufas. Whether the usual hearth, in form of a basin, and the wall beside it, had been constructed here I was unfortunately unable to determine, more than half of the room being filled with rubbish. I give the name of estufas to these square rooms with rounded corners, built as described above, because they are furnished with the passage characteristic of the round estufas in the cliff-dwellings. Perhaps they mark the transition to the rectangular estufa of the Moki Indians. Besides the estufas there are some other round rooms or towers (21 a, 23, 63), which evidently belonged to the fortifications of the village. They differ from the estufas in the absence of the characteristic passage and also of the six niches. Furthermore, they often contain several stories, and in every respect but the form resemble the rectangular rooms. The long wall just mentioned, built on a narrow ledge above the other ruins, and visible at the top of Pl. XIII was probably another part of the village fortifications. The ledge is situated so near the roof of the cave that the wall, though quite low, touches the latter, and the only way of advancing behind it is to creep on hands and knees.

A comparison between Pl. VIII and Pl. XIII shows at once that the inhabitants of the Cliff Palace were further advanced in architecture than their more western kinsfolk on the Mesa Verde. The stones are carefully dressed and often laid in regular courses; the walls are perpendicular, sometimes leaning slightly inwards at the same angle all round the room—this being part of the design. All the corners form almost perfect right angles, when the surroundings have permitted the builders to observe this rule. This remark also applies to the doorways, the sides of which are true and even. The lintel often consists of

---

[a] A part of this wall may be seen to the extreme right of Pl. XIII, and also in fig. 34 behind and to the right of the tower.

a large stone slab, extending right across the opening. On closer observation
we find that in the Cliff Palace we may discriminate two slightly different
methods of building. The lower walls, where the stones are only rough-hewn
and laid without order, are often surmounted by walls of carefully dressed
blocks in regular courses. This circumstance suggests that the cave was
inhabited during two different periods. I shall have occasion below to return
to this question.

The rooms of the Cliff Palace seem to have been better provided with light
and air than the cliff-dwellings in general, small peep-holes appearing at
several places in the walls. The doorways, as in other cliff-dwellings, are
either rectangular or T-shaped. Some of the latter are of unusual size, in
one instance 1.05 m. high and 0.81 m. broad at the top. The thickness of the
walls is generally about 0.3 m., sometimes, in the outer walls, as much as 0.6 m.
As a rule they are not painted, but in some rooms covered with a thin coat of
yellow plaster. At the south end of the ruin lies an estufa (93) which is
well-preserved (fig. 37). This estufa is entered by a doorway in the wall,
one of the few instances where I have observed this arrangement. In most
cases, as I have already mentioned, the entrance was probably constructed in
the roof. The dimensions of this estufa were as follows: diameter 3.9 m.,
distance from the floor to the bottom of the niches 1.2 m., height of the niches
0.9 m., breadth of the same 1.3 m., depth of the same 0.5 to 1.3 m., height of
the passage at its mouth 0.75 m., breadth of the same 0.45 m. Five small
quadrangular holes or niches were scattered here and there in the lower part
of the wall.

I cannot refrain from once more laying stress on the skill to which the walls
of Cliff Palace in general bear witness, and the stability and strength which has
been supplied to them by the careful dressing of the blocks and the chinking
of the interstices with small chips of stone. A point remarked by Jackson in
his description of the ruins of Southwestern Colorado, is that the finger marks
of the mason may still be traced in the mortar, and that those marks are so
small as to suggest that the work of building was performed by women. This
conclusion seems too hasty, for within the range of my observations the size of
the finger marks varies not a little.

Like Sprucetree House and other large ruins the Cliff Palace contains at
the back of the cave extensive open spaces where tame turkeys were probably
kept. In this part of the village three small rooms, isolated from the rest of
the building, occupy a position close to the cliff; two of them (103, 104), built
of large flat slabs of stones, lie close together, the third (105), of unhewn
sandstone (fig. 38), is situated farther north. These rooms may serve as
examples of the most primitive form of architecture among the cliff people.

In the Cliff Palace, the rooms lie on different levels, the ground occupied by
them being very rough. In several places terraces have been constructed in
order to procure a level foundation, and here as in their other architectural
labours, the cliff-dwellers have displayed considerable skill.

One very remarkable circumstance in the Cliff Palace is that all the pieces of
timber, all the large rafters, have disappeared. The holes where they passed
into the walls may still be seen, but throughout the great block of ruins two
or three large beams are all that remain. This is the reason why none of the
rooms is completely closed. At Sprucetree House there were a number of
rooms where the placing of the door stone in position was enough to throw the
room into perfect darkness, no little aid to the execution of photographic work.
It is difficult to explain the above state of things. I observed the same want of
timber in parts of other ruins (at Long House for example). In several of
the cliff-dwellings it appears as if the beams had purposely been removed from

the walls to be applied to some other use. Seldom, however, have all the rafters disappeared, as in the Cliff Palace. There are no traces of the ravages of fire. Perhaps the inhabitants were forced, during the course of a siege, to use the timber as fuel; but in that case it is difficult to understand how a proportionate supply of provisions and water was obtained. This is one of the numerous circumstances which are probably connected with the extinction or migration of the former inhabitants, but from which our still scanty information of the cliff-dwellers cannot lift the veil of obscurity.

In addition to his description Nordenskiöld gives a ground plan of Cliff Palace[a] (pl. xi); a magnificent double page view of the ruin from the west (pl. xiii); a fine picture of Speaker-chief's House (pl. xii); a view of the Round Tower (fig. 34); a figure and a plan of an estufa of singular construction (T); a view of the interior of Kiva C and of a small room at the back of the main rows of rooms. No specimens of pottery, stone implements, and kindred antiquities from Cliff Palace are figured by Nordenskiöld. In various places throughout his work this author refers to Cliff Palace in a comparative way, and in his descriptions of other ruins the student will find more or less pertaining to it.

In his book The Cliff Dwellers and Pueblos,[b] Rev. Stephen D. Peet devotes one chapter (VII) to Cliff Palace and its surroundings, compiling and quoting from Chapin, Birdsall, and Nordenskiöld. No new data appear in this work, and the illustrations are copied from these authors.

Dr. Edgar L. Hewett[c] briefly refers to Cliff Palace as follows (p. 54):

Il suffira de décrire les traits principaux d'un seul groupement de ruines, et nous choisirons Cliff Palace, qui en est le spécimen le plus remarquable (pl. i b). Il est situé dans un bras de *Ruin Canyon*. La vue présentée ici est prise d'un point plus elévé, au sud, d'ou l'on contemple les ruines d'une ville ancienne, avec des tours rondes et carrées, des maisons, des entrepôts pour le grain, des habitations et des lieux de culte. Le Cliff Palace remplit une immense caverne bien défendue et à l'abri des ravages des éléments. Un sentier conduit aux ruines. Le plan (Fig. 2) représente les restes de 105 chambres au plain-pied. On ne sait combien il y en avait dans les 3 étages supérieurs, mais il est probable que Cliff-Palace n'abritait pas moins de 500 personnes.

Nous remarquons à Cliff-Palace de grands progrés dans l'art de la construction. Les murs sont faits de grés gris, taillé avec des outils de pierre, dont on voit encore les traces. Lorsqu'on se servait de pierres irrégulières, les crevasses étaient remplies avec des fragments ou des éclats de grés, puis on plâtrait les murs avec du mortier d'adobe. On prenait de grosses poutres pour les plafonds et les planchers, et l'on peut voir que ces poutres étaient dégrossies avec des instruments peu tranchants.

---

[a] The illustrations referred to in this paragraph are in Nordenskiöld's work.

[b] As stated in a note (Peet, p. 133) Chapter VII is a reprint of Doctor Birdsall's article in the *Journal of the American Geographical Society*, op. cit.

[c] In Les Communautés Anciennes dans le Désert Américain. In this work may be found a ground plan of Cliff Palace by Morley and Kidder, the interior of kiva Q (pl. viii, e), and a large view of the ruin taken from the north (pl. i, b). (Plate and figure designations from Hewett.)

Many newspaper and magazine accounts of the Mesa Verde ruins appeared about the time Mr. Chapin's description was published, but the majority of these are somewhat distorted and more or less exaggerated, often too indefinite for scientific purposes. References to them, even if here quoted, could hardly be of great value to the reader, as in most cases it would be impossible for him to consult files of papers in which they occur even if the search were worth while. Much that they record is practically a compilation from previous descriptions.

The activity in photographing Cliff Palace has done much to make known its existence and structure. Many excellent photographs of the ruin have been taken, among which may be mentioned those of Chapin, Nordenskiöld, Vreeland, Nusbaum, and others. Oil paintings, some of which are copied from photographs, others made from the ruin itself, adorn the walls of some of our museums. Almost every visitor to the Mesa Verde carries with him a camera, and many good postal cards with views of the ruin are on the market. Negatives of Cliff Palace taken before its excavation and repair will become more valuable as time passes, because they can no longer be duplicated. From a study of a considerable number of these photographs it seems that very little change has taken place in the condition of the ruin between the time the first pictures were made and the repair work was begun.

SITE OF CLIFF PALACE

Cliff Palace is situated in a cave in Cliff-palace canyon, a branch of Cliff canyon, which is here about 200 feet deep. It occupies practically the whole of the cave, the roof of which overhangs about two-thirds of the ruin, projecting considerably beyond its middle. This cave is much more capacious than that in which Spruce-tree House is situated, as shown by comparing illustrations and descriptions of the latter in the former report. The configuration of Spruce-tree House cave and that of Cliff Palace, and the relation of its floor to the talus, also differ. The canyon in which Cliff Palace lies is thickly wooded, having many cedars and a few pines and scrub oaks; the almost total failure of water at certain seasons of the year at Cliff Palace renders floral life in the vicinity less exuberant than in Spruce-tree canyon, a branch of Navaho canyon (fig. 1). On the level plateau above the ruin there are many trees—pines and cedars—but even this area is not so thickly wooded as the summit of the mesa above Spruce-tree House.[a]

---

[a] Clearings in the forest indicate the positions of the former farms of the inhabitants of Cliff Palace.

The geological formation of the cave in which Cliff Palace is situated is similar to that at Spruce-tree House, consisting of alternating layers of hard and soft sandstone, shale, and even layers of coal. Both canyons and caves appear to have been formed by the same processes. In past ages the elements have eroded and undermined the soft layers of sandstone or shale to such an extent that great blocks of rock, being left without foundations, have broken away from above, falling down the precipice. Many of these great bowlders remained on the floor of a cave where it was broad enough to retain them. The surface of the roof arching over Cliff Palace cave is perhaps smoother than that of Spruce-tree House. The progress of cave erosion was greatly augmented by the flow of water from the mesa summit during heavy rains, as hereinafter described.

To understand the general plan of Cliff Palace it is necessary to take into consideration the method of formation and the configuration of the cave

FIG. 1.—View down Navaho Canyon.

floor on which the ruin stands. This cave, as already stated, was formed by erosion or undercutting the softer rock at a lower level than the massive sandstone, leaving huge blocks of stone above the eroded cavities. Naturally these blocks, being without support, fell, and in falling were broken, the larger fragments remaining on the floor practically in the places where they fell, but many of the smaller stones were washed out of the cave entrance, forming a talus extending down the side of the cliff. The floor of the cave was thus strewn with stones, large and small, resting on the same general level which is that on which the foundations of the buildings were constructed. The level of the cave floor was interrupted by the huge blocks of stone forming its outer margin; and the buildings constructed on these fallen rocks were lofty, even imposing. The talus composed of fallen rock and débris, piled against the canyon side in front of these buildings and below these huge blocks of stone, extends many feet down the cliff in a gradual slope, covering the terraced buildings and burying their retaining walls from sight.[a] A great part of this talus is composed of fallen walls, but considerable earth and small stones are contained in it, probably precipitated over the rim of the cave roof by the torrents of water which sometimes fall during heavy rains. It is probable also that the foresting of the talus has been due more or less to bushes and small trees washed over the cliff from the mesa summit.

Three terraces or tiers containing rooms, as shown in the accompanying ground plan, were revealed by excavations in this talus. At the western extension, where the second and third terraces cease, the tops of large rocks begin at the level of the fourth terrace, and on the southern end the first terrace is absent. At the western extremity, the large blocks of rock having dropped down entire from the side of the cliff, fill the interval elsewhere occupied by the lower terraces, and their tops now form a ledge upon which rest the foundations of rooms level with the plaza. It is thus evident that whereas the front wall of Spruce-tree House is simple, the level of the kiva roofs and floors of buildings above ground being continuous, the front of Cliff Palace is complicated, being at different levels, consisting of terraces in the talus. As one aproached Cliff Palace, when inhabited, it must have presented, from below, an imposing structure, the lower terraces being occupied by many large kivas above which rose lofty buildings arranged in tiers, several being four stories high. Although the height was much increased by the presence of huge foundation blocks of sandstone, from the lowest terrace to the highest room there were seven floor levels, including those of the kivas in the terraces.

An examination of Cliff Palace cave shows that from the southern end to the section over the main entrance its roof arches upward and that the part over the rear of the ruin is lower than that over its front. Between the lower and upper roof levels there is a sharp break formed by a vertical cleavage plane. Where this plane joins the upper level there is a shelf forming a recess in which has been constructed a row of ledge rooms.[b]

The great rock roof arching over Cliff Palace is broken about midway between the vertical plane above mentioned and the rim by another and narrower vertical plane where no ledge exists. Here multitudes of swallows had made their home, and there are wasps' nests in several places.

---

[a] Access to Cliff Palace from the bottom of the canyon, although difficult, is possible, and a pathway might be constructed down its sides or along the top of the talus to several other cliff-dwellings. In the vicinity of Cliff Palace there are at least 20 ruins, large and small.

[b] One of these rooms had been chosen by eagles for their nests, but both nests and eggs were abandoned by the birds after the repair work was begun.

PREHISTORIC TRAILS TO CLIFF PALACE

It is evident that the prehistoric farmers of Cliff Palace repeatedly visited their fields among the cedars on top of the mesa, and well-worn trails led from their habitation to these clearings. Several such trails have long been known, one of which was formerly exclusively used by white visitors and was facetiously called "Fat Man's Misery." To another ancient pathway, near which ladders were placed, the name "Ladder Trail" may be applied. The pathways now used by visitors follow approximately these old trails, which were simply series of shallow footholes cut in the cliff. Although the lapse of time since they were pecked in the rock has somewhat diminished their depth, they can still be used by an adventurous climber.

GENERAL FEATURES

Cliff Palace (pls. 1, 2), the most instructive cliff-house yet discovered in the Mesa Verde National Park, if not in the United States, is one of the most picturesque ruins in the Southwest. While its general contour follows that of the rear of the cave in which it is situated, its two extremities project beyond the cavern. The entire central part is protected by the cave roof; the ends are exposed.

The general orientation of Cliff Palace is north and south, the cave lying at the eastern end of the canyon of which it is an extension. The southern end is practically outside this cave, and the few rooms westward from kiva V are unprotected. An isolated kiva, W, with high surrounding walls, is situated some distance beyond the extreme western end of the ruin. Although not in the same cave as the main ruin, certain other rooms in the vicinity of Cliff Palace may have been ceremonially connected with it. They are built in shallow depressions in the cliffs and may have been shrines or rooms to which priests retreated for the purpose of performing their rites. In the category of dependent structures may also be mentioned numerous rings of stones on top of the mesa. The existence of calcined human bones in the soil over which these stones are heaped indicates the practice of cremation, of which there is also evidence in the ruin itself.

DESTRUCTION BY THE ELEMENTS

The constant beating of rain and snow, often accompanied in winter by freezing of water in the crevices of the masonry, has sadly dilapidated a large part of the front walls of Cliff Palace, especially those at the northern and southern ends (pl. 3) where they do not have the protection of the overhanging roof of the cave.

While the sections known as the old quarter, the plaza quarter, and much of the tower quarter are protected by the roof of the cave, even here there has been exposure and destruction from the same cause. Torrential rains on the mesa in the late summer form streams of water which, following depressions,[a] flow over the rim of the cave roof and are precipitated into the trees beyond the lowest terrace of the ruin. The destruction of walls from these flows is much less than that from smaller streams which, following the edge of the cave roof, run under the roof and drip on the walls, washing the mortar from between the component stones, and eventually undermining their foundation and leading to their fall. The former presence of these streams is indicated by the black discoloration of the cave roof shown in photographs.

A visitor to Cliff Palace in the dry season can hardly imagine the amount of rain that occasionally falls during the summer months, and it is difficult for him to appreciate the destructive force it exerts when precipitated over the cliff. When Cliff Palace was occupied, damage to walls could be immediately repaired by the inhabitants after every torrent, but as the ruin remained for centuries uninhabited and without repair, the extent of the destruction was great. The torrents falling over the ruin not only gain force from the distance of the fall, but sweep everything before them, bringing down earth, stones, small trees, and bushes. At such a time the bottom of the canyon is filled with a roaring torrent fed by waterfalls that can be seen at intervals far down the gorge. The observer standing in Cliff Palace during such a downpour can behold a sheet of water falling over the projecting cliff in front of him. These cataracts fortunately are never of long duration, but while they last their power is irresistible.[b]

VANDALISM

No ruin in the Mesa Verde Park had suffered more from the ravages of "pot hunters" than Cliff Palace; indeed it had been much more mutilated than the other ruins in the park (pls. 1, 4, 5). Parties of workmen had remained at the ruin all winter, and many specimens had been taken from it and sold. There was good evidence that the workmen had wrenched beams from the roofs and floors to use for firewood, so that not a single roof and but few rafters remained in place. However, no doubt many of the beams had been

---

[a] In some of these waterways are found good examples of "potholes," some of considerable size, which often retain water for a long time. Their capacity was increased in prehistoric times by the construction of dams.

[b] While there has probably been considerable erosion in the bed of the canyon since Cliff Palace was constructed, this does not mean that "the action of the water carved out the valley, leaving at an inaccessible height buildings originally constructed on almost level land." See History N. Y. State Chapter, Colorado Cliff Dwellings Assoc., p. 11.

removed, possibly by cliff-dwellers, long before white men first visited the place.

Many of the walls had been broken down and their foundations undermined, leaving great rents through them to let in light or to allow passage from the débris thrown in the rooms as dumping places. Hardly a floor had not been dug into, and some of the finest walls had been demolished.[a] All this was done to obtain pottery and other minor antiquities that had a market value. The arrest of this vandalism is fortunate and shows an awakened public sentiment, but it can not repair the irreparable harm that has been done.

REPAIR OF WALLS

The masonry work necessary to repair a ruin as large and as much demolished as Cliff Palace was very considerable. The greatest amount was expended on those walls in front of the cave floor hidden under the lower terraces, at the northern and southern extremities. The latter portion was so completely destroyed that it had to be rebuilt in some places, while at the southern end an equal amount of repair work was necessary. (Pls. 3, 6, 7, 9.) To permanently protect these sections of the ruin the tops of the walls and the plazas were liberally covered with Portland cement, and runways were constructed to carry off the surface water into gutters by which it was diverted over the retaining walls to fall on the rock foundations beyond. It would be impossible permanently to protect some of these exposed walls without constructing roofs above them; at present every heavy rain is bound to cover the floors of the kivas with water and thus eventually to undermine their foundations.

The preservation of walls deep in the cave under protection of the roof was not a difficult problem. The work in this part consisted chiefly in the repair of kiva walls, building them to their former height at the level of neighboring plazas.

MAJOR ANTIQUITIES

Under this term are embraced those immovable objects as walls of houses and their various structural parts—floors, roofs, and fireplaces. These features must of necessity be protected in place and left where they were constructed. Minor antiquities, as implements of various kinds, stone objects, pottery, textiles, and the like, can best be removed and preserved in a museum, where they can be seen to greater advantage and by a much larger number of people. The ideal way would be to preserve both major and minor antiquities

---

[a] Some, possibly considerable, of this mutilation may be ascribed to the former occupants. The Ute Indians will not now enter cliff-dwellings and probably are not responsible for their destruction.

together in the same neighborhood, or to install the latter in the places in which they were found. While at present such an arrangement at Spruce-tree House and Cliff Palace is not practicable, large specimens, as metates and those jars that are embedded in the walls, have, as a rule, been left as they were found.

As the repair work at Cliff Palace was limited to the protection of the major antiquities, the smaller objects for the greater part having been removed before our work began, this report deals more especially with the former, the whole ruin being regarded as a great specimen to be preserved in situ.

Very little attention was given to labeling rooms, kivas, and their different parts, the feeling being that this experiment has been sufficiently well carried out at Spruce-tree House, an examination of which would logically precede that of Cliff Palace. Spruce-tree House has been made a " type ruin " from which the tourist can gain his first impression of the major antiquities of the Mesa Verde National Park, and while it was well to indicate on its walls the different features characteristic of these buildings, it would be redundant to carry out the same plan in the other ruins.[a]

No attempt was made to restore the roof of any of the Cliff Palace kivas for the reason that one can gain a good idea of how the roof of a circular kiva is constructed from its restoration in Kiva C of Spruce-tree House, and an effort to roof a kiva of Cliff Palace would merely duplicate what has already been accomplished without adding essentially to our knowledge.

GENERAL PLAN OF CLIFF PALACE

The ground plans of Cliff Palace which have been published were made from surface indications before excavations were undertaken and necessarily do not represent all the rooms. Nordenskiöld's map outlines 17 kivas and 102 rooms, indicating several kivas by dotted lines. The Morley-Kidder map, which represents positions of 18 or 19 kivas, notes 105 secular rooms.[b] Although this ground plan is an improvement on that of Nordenskiöld, it also was based on surface indications and naturally fails to indicate those kivas that were buried under the fallen walls of the terraces. Strangely enough, in Nordenskiöld's ground plan Kiva K is omitted, notwithstanding the tops of one or two pilasters were readily seen before any excavation was

---

[a] The author's hope is to excavate and repair in different sections of the Southwest a number of " type ruins," each of which will illustrate the major antiquities of the area in which it occurs. From an examination of these types the tourist and the student may obtain, at first hand, an accurate knowledge of the prehistoric architecture.

[b] In " Report, House of Representatives, No. 3703, 58th Congress," Mr. Coert Dubois ascribes to Cliff House (Cliff Palace) 146 rooms and 5 estufas (kivas). Unfortunately the error in the count of kivas has been given wide circulation. As stated in the present article, there are at least 23 rooms in Cliff Palace that may be called kivas.

made. Neither of these plans distinguishes those buildings that have more than a single story, although they show the parts of walls that extend to the roof. Neither Chapin nor Birdsall published maps of Cliff Palace. (See pl. 8.)

TERRACES AND RETAINING WALLS

The terraces in front of the rooms occupying the floor of the cave are characteristic features of Cliff Palace (pls. 9, 10). The excavations revealed three of these terraces, of which the floor of the cave is the fourth. This fourth terrace, or cave floor, is in the main horizontal, but on account of the accumulated talus the slope from the southern end of the portion in front of kiva G was gradual and continued at about this level to the northern end of the ruin. This slope brought it about that kivas in the terraces are at different levels. The floors of kivas H and I lie on about the level of the first terrace, that of G on the terrace above, and F lies on the third terrace; the remaining kivas are all excavated in the cave floor, or fourth terrace. From the main entrance to the ruin, extending northward, there are representations of the second and third terraces, both of which extend to the cliff in front of kiva U. It is probable from the general appearance of the ruin that when all the terraces and walls were intact Cliff Palace was also terraced with houses along the front, which recalls architectural features in certain cliff-dwellings in Canyon de Chelly.

TOWER QUARTER

For convenience of description Cliff Palace is arbitrarily divided into four quarters, known as tower quarter, plaza quarter, old quarter, and northern quarter. The tower quarter (pls. 10–14) occupies the whole southern portion of the ruin and extends to the extreme southern end from a line drawn perpendicular to the cliff through the round tower. It includes 8 kivas, A to G, and J, 6 of which, A, B, C, D, E, and J, are situated on the fourth terrace, the level of the kiva floor being that of the third terrace. Kiva F lies in the third, and G in the second terrace. It will be seen from an inspection of the ground plan that there are in all 29 rooms in this quarter, besides the 8 kivas, an instructive fact when compared with Spruce-tree House with its 8 kivas and 114 rooms. It must be remembered that several of the rooms in this quarter are of two stories, one is of three stories, and one of four stories, thus adding from 15 to 20 rooms to the 8 enumerated as occupying the ground floor. The proportion of ceremonial rooms to kivas in this quarter would be a little more than 2 to 1.

PLAZA QUARTER

The plaza quarter, as its name indicates, is a large open space, the floor of which is formed mainly by the contiguous roofs of the several kivas (K to O) that are sunk below it. The main entrance to the village opens into this plaza at its northwestern corner, and on the northern side it is continued into a court which connects with the main street or alley of the cliff village. From its position, relations, and other considerations, it is supposed that this quarter was an important section of Cliff Palace and that here were held some of the large open-air gatherings of the inhabitants of the place; here also no doubt were celebrated the sacred dances which we have every reason to believe were at times performed by the former inhabitants. The roof levels of kivas H and I did not contribute to the size of the main plaza, but show good evidence of later construction. Judging from the number of fireplaces in this quarter there is reason to believe that much cooking was done in this open space, in addition to its use for ceremonial or other gatherings of the inhabitants.

OLD QUARTER

The section of Cliff Palace that has been designated the old quarter (pls. 14, 15) lies between a line drawn from the main entrance of the ruin to the rear of the cave and the extreme northern end, culminating in a high castle-like cluster of rooms. It may well be called one of the most important sections of Cliff Palace, containing, as it does, the largest number of rooms, the most varied architecture, and the best masonry. Its protected situation under the roof of the cave is such that we may consider it and the adjoining plaza quarter the earliest settled sections of the village. It contains all varieties of inclosures known in cliff-dwellings: kivas of two types, round rooms, rectangular rooms, an alley or a street, and a court. The floor of the cave on which the rooms are built is broadest at this point, which is one of the best protected sites and the least accessible to enemies in the whole building. It may be theoretically supposed that originally the kiva quarter was an annex of this section and that some of the kivas in this quarter may also have been owned and used by the clans which founded Cliff Palace. The old quarter is divided into two parts, a northern and a southern, the former being arbitrarily designated the Speaker-chief's House. The "street" running approximately north and south bisects the old quarter, making a front and a rear section.

NORTHERN QUARTER

This quarter (pl. 16) of Cliff Palace extends from the high rocks on which the Speaker-chief's House is perched, in a westerly direction, ending with a milling room and adjacent inclosures 92 to 94, situated

west of kiva V.   It includes three kivas; two, U and V, being situated
on the fourth terrace; and one, T, on the first terrace.   Kivas U and
V are built on top of large rocks, the floor of kiva V being excavated
in solid rock.   Much of this quarter, especially the western end, is
under the sky, and consequently without the protection of the cave
roof, on which account it was considerably destroyed by rain water
flowing over the canyon rim.   The walls of this quarter, especially
where it joins the old quarter, exhibit fine masónry, suggesting that
it was inhabited by important clans.

MASONRY

The walls of Cliff Palace present the finest masonry known to any
cliff-dwelling and among the best stonework in prehistoric ruins
north of Mexico.   A majority of the stones used in the construction
were well dressed before laying and smoothed after they were set in
the wall.   The joints are often broken, but it is rare to find intersect-
ing walls or corners bonded.   Stones of approximately the same size
are employed, thereby making the courses, as a rule, level.   Although
commonly the foundations are composed of the largest stones, this
is not an invariable rule, often larger stones being laid above
smaller ones; the latter, even when used for foundations, are sometimes set on edge.   As a rule, the walls are not plumb or straight.
The custom of laying stone foundations on wooden beams is shown in
several instances, especially in cases where it was necessary to bridge
the intervals between projecting rocks.   The arch was unknown to
the masons of Cliff Palace; there are no pillars to support floors or
roofs as in Spruce-tree House.   It is not rare, especially in the kivas,
to find instances of double or reenforced walls which may or may not
be bonded by connecting stones.

The masonry of the kivas as a rule is superior to that of the secular
rooms.   The mortar employed in the construction is hard; the joints
are chinked with spalls, fragments of pottery, or clay balls.   The
fact that much more mortar than was necessary was employed resulted
in weakening the walls.   Several walls were laid without mortar; in
some of these the joints were pointed, in others not.[a]   The ancient
builders did not always seek solid bases for foundations, but built
their walls in several instances on ashes or sand, evidently not
knowing when the foundations were laid that other stories would
later be constructed upon them.

In several sections of the ruin there are evidences that old walls,
apparently of houses formerly used, served in part as walls for new
buildings.   There are also several instances of secondary construction

---

[a] Fragments of mortar from the walls and floors, ground to powder, were used in the
repair work.

in which old entrances are walled up or even buried and old passageways covered with new structures. Similar reconstruction is common
in Hopi pueblos, where it has led to enlargement of rooms and other
variations in form. Among the several examples of such secondary
building in Cliff Palace may be mentioned a long wall, evidently
the front of a large building, which serves as a rear wall of several
rooms arranged side by side. The obvious explanation of such a condition is that the walls of the small rooms are of later construction.

As above mentioned the foundations of many walls are of larger
stones, and the masonry here is coarser than higher up, which has
led some authors to ascribe this fact as due to two epochs of construction. But this conclusion does not appear to be wholly justifiable,
although there is evidence in many places that there has been rebuilding over old walls and consequent modification in new con-
structions, by which older walls have ceased to be necessary, a condition not unlike that existing in several of the Hopi pueblos. In
this category may be included the several doors and windows that
have been filled in with new masonry or even concealed by new walls.
From the fragile character of certain foundations of high walls it
would appear that it was not the intention, when they were laid, to
erect on them walls more than one story high; the construction of
higher stories upon them was an afterthought. Evidences occur of
repair of breaks in the walls and corners by the aboriginal occupants,
one of the most apparent of which appears at the end of the court
in the southern wall of room 59.

Adobe Bricks

The walls, as a rule, were made of stone; indeed it is unusual to find
adobe walls in cliff-dwellings of the Mesa Verde. In prehistoric
buildings in our Southwest, evidences that the ancients made adobe
bricks, sun-dried before laying, are very rare. Bricks made of clay
are set in the walls of the Speaker-chief's House and were found in
the fallen débris at its base. These bricks were made cubical in form
before laying, but there is nothing to prove that they were molded
in forms or frames, nor do they have a core of straw as in the case
of the adobes used in the construction of Inscription House in the
Navaho National Monument, Arizona.[a] The use af adobes in the construction of cliff-house walls has not been previously mentioned,
although we find references to "lumps of clay" in the earliest historic times among Pueblos. Thus the inhabitants of Tiguex, according to Castañeda, were acquainted with adobes. "They collect," says
this author, "great heaps of thyme and rushes and set them on fire;
when the mass is reduced to ashes and charcoal they cast a great

---

a See *Bulletin 50, Bureau of American Ethnology.*

quantity of earth and water upon it and mix the whole together. They knead this stuff into round lumps, which they learn to dry and use instead of stone."

Attention may be called to the fact that not only the adobes found at Cliff Palace but also the mortar used in the construction of the walls contain ashes and sometimes even small fragments of charcoal. Clay or adobe plastered on osiers woven between upright sticks, so common in the walls of cliff-dwellings in Canyon de Chelly and in the ruins in the Navaho Monument, while not unknown in the Mesa Verde, is an exceptional method of construction and was not observed at Cliff Palace. The survival [a] of this method of building a wall, if survival it be, may be seen in the deflector of kiva K.

PLASTERING

The walls of a number of rooms were coated with a layer of plastering of sand or clay. This was found on the outside of some walls, where it is generally worn, but it is best preserved on the interior surfaces. Perhaps the most striking examples of plastering on exterior walls occurs on the Speaker-chief's House, where the smoothness of the finish is noteworthy.

From impressions of hands and fingers on this plastering it is evident that it was laid on not with trowels but with the hands, and as the impressions of hands are small the plasterers were probably women or children. In several instances where the plastering is broken several successive layers are seen, often in different colors, sometimes separated by a thin black layer deposited by smoke. The color of the plastering varies considerably, sometimes showing red, often yellow or white, depending on the different colored sand or mud employed.[b] The plastering not only varies in color but also in thickness and in finish. In the most protected rooms of the cave practically all the superficial plastering still remains on both the interior and the exterior of the walls, but for the greater part it has been washed from the surfaces and out of the joints in the outer buildings. The mortar was evidently rubbed smooth with the hands, aided, perhaps, with flat stones. The exterior of one or two rooms shows several coats of plaster, and different parts of the same walls are of different

[a] In at least one of the Oraibi kivas the plastering of the wall is laid on sticks that form a kind of lathing. Whether this is a survival of an older method of construction or is traceable to European influence has not been determined, but it is believed to be a survival of prehistoric wall construction.

[b] The red color is derived from the red soil common everywhere on the mesa. Yellow was obtained from disintegrated rock, and white is a marl which is found at various places. The mortar used by the ancient masons became harder, almost cement, when made of marl mixed with adobe.

colors. Indistinct figures are scratched on several walls, but the majority of these are too obscure to be traced or deciphered. The plastering on the exterior and the interior of the same wall is often of different color.

PAINTINGS AND ROCK MARKINGS

Figures are painted on the white plastering of the third story of room 11 and on the lower border of the banquette of kiva I, the former being the most elaborate mural paintings known in cliff-dwellings, showing several symbols which are reproduced on pottery. A reversed symbolic rain-cloud figure, painted white, occurs on the exterior of the low ledge house.[a] Mural paintings of unusual form are found on the under side of the projecting rock forming part of the floor of room 3, and there are scratches on the plastering of the wall of kiva K. The latter figures were intended to represent animals, heads of grotesque beings, possibly birds, and terraced designs symbolic of rain clouds. As one or more of these symbols occur on pottery fragments, there appears no doubt that both were made by the same people. Among rock markings may also be mentioned shallow, concave grooves made by rubbing harder stones, which can be seen on the cliffs in front of rooms 92 and 93 and in the court west of room 51.

Among the figures painted on whitewashed walls of room 11 may be mentioned triangles, parallel red lines with dots, and a square figure, in red, crossed by zigzags, recalling the designs on old Navaho blankets.

The parallel lines are placed vertically and are not unlike, save in color, those which the Hopi make with prayer meal on the walls of their kivas, in certain ceremonies. But it is to be noted that the Hopi markings are made horizontally instead of vertically, as at Cliff Palace. The dots represented on the sides of some of these parallel lines (room 11) are similar to those appearing on straight lines or triangles in the decoration of Mesa Verde pottery. The triangular figures still used by the Hopi in decorating the margins of dados in their houses also occur on some of the Cliff-Palace walls, but are placed in a reversed position. They are said to represent a butterfly, a rain cloud, or a sex symbol. It is interesting to note in passing that two or more triangles placed one above another appear constantly in the same position in Moorish tile and stucco decorations, but this, of course, is only a coincidence, as there is no evidence of a cultural connection.

---

[a] This figure resembles closely that on the outside walls of the third story of room 11 of Spruce-tree House. (See pls. 4, 5, 6, *Bulletin 41, Bureau of American Ethnology*.)

Refuse Heaps

Almost every Mesa Verde cliff-dwelling has an unoccupied space back of the rooms,[a] as in the rear of rooms 28 to 40, which served as a depository for all kinds of rubbish. Here the inhabitants of Cliff Palace also deposited certain of their dead, which became mummified on account of the dryness of the air in the cave.

There is also a vacant space between the rear of the Speaker-chief's House and the cave wall, but this space was almost entirely free of refuse. The amount of débris in the refuse heaps back of the so-called plaza quarter lends weight to other evidence that this is one of the oldest sections of Cliff Palace.

The accumulation of débris was so deep in these places, and the difficulties of removal so great, that it was not attempted. It had all been dug over by relic seekers who are said to have found many specimens therein.[b]

Secular Rooms

The majority of the rooms in Cliff Palace were devoted to secular purposes. These are of several types, and differ in form, in position, and in function. Their form is either circular or rectangular, or some modification of these two. As a rule, the secular rooms lie deep under the cliffs, several extending as far back as the rear of the cave. The front of Cliff Palace shows at least two tiers or terraces of secular rooms, the roof of the lower one being level with that of the floor of the tier above. The front walls of secular rooms lower than the fourth terrace are as a rule destroyed, but the lateral walls are evident, especially in the tower quarter. The passage from one of these terraces to the room above was made by means of ladders or by stone steps along the corners.

The following classification of secular rooms, based on their function, may be noted: (1) Living rooms; (2) milling rooms; (3) storage rooms; (4) rooms of unknown function;[c] (5) towers; (6) round

---

[a] Isolated cliff-dwellings are scattered throughout the Southwest, but there are several areas, as the Mesa Verde, in which they are concentrated. Among these clusters may be mentioned the Canyon de Chelly, the Navaho National Monument, the Red Rocks area, and that of the upper Gila. One characteristic feature in which the cliff-dwellings of the Mesa Verde differ from some others is the independence of all of the upright walls from support of the sides of the cliffs. In the cliff-houses of the Navaho Monument a large majority of the houses have the rear wall of the cave as a wall of the building; a few of the houses in Cliff Palace have the same, but the largest number are entirely free from the cliff. This separation on all sides is due largely to the geological structure of the rear of the cavern in which the cliff-house stands.

[b] Workmen could operate in these parts only by tying sponges over their nostrils, so difficult was it to breathe on account of the fine dust.

[c] Possibly some of these may have been used sometimes for ceremonial purposes, or rather for the less important rites.

rooms. It is difficult to distinguish in some instances to which of the above classes some of the rooms belong. The secular houses were probably owned by the oldest women of the clan, and the kivas were the property of the men of their respective clans, but courts, plazas, and pasageways were common property.

The masonry[a] of all secular rooms is practically identical and as a rule is inferior to that of kivas, their walls varying in width and having a uniform thickness from foundation to top. There are instances where the lower part projects somewhat beyond the upper, from which it is separated by a ledge, but this feature is not common. Minor features of architecture, as floors and roofs, doors and windows, fireplaces, banks, and cubby-holes, some or all of which may be absent, vary in form and in distribution according to the purpose for which the room was intended. The few timbers that remain show that the beams of the houses were probably cut with stone hatchets aided by the use of fire. The labor of hauling these timbers and of stripping them of their branches must have been great, considering the rude appliances at hand. It would seem that the cliff-dwellers were not ignorant of the use of the wedge with which to split logs, since the surfaces of split sticks are always more or less fibrous, never smooth, as would be expected if metal implements had been used. All transportation was manual, without the assistance of beasts of burden or of any but the rudest mechanical contrivances.

Doors and Windows

There is difficulty in distinguishing doorways from windows in cliff-dwellings, on which account they are here treated together. Both are simple openings in the walls, the former as a rule being larger than the latter. As door openings are regularly situated high above the floor, there may have been ladders by which the doorways of the second and third stories were reached. The rooms may have been entered by means of balconies, evidences of which still remain. No instance of a hatchway in the roof is now recognizable, although the absence of side entrances in several rooms implies that there were roof entrances, several good examples of which occur at Spruce-tree House.

Doorways of Cliff Palace have two forms, rectangular and T-shaped, the latter generally opening on the second story or in such a position that they were approached by ladders or notched logs. The theory that these doorways were constructed larger at the top than at the bottom so that persons with packs on their backs might

---

[a] Probably both men and women of one clan worked together in the construction of houses, the men being the masons, the women the plasterers. Each clan built its own rooms, and there were no differentiated groups of mechanics in the community.

pass through them more readily is not wholly satisfactory, nor does the theory that the notch at the lower rim served to keep the ladder from slipping wholly commend itself. No satisfactory explanation of the form of the T-shaped doorway has been yet determined. Generally the tops of both doorways and windows are narrower than the bottoms, the sides being slightly inclined; but the lower part is rarely narrower than the top. Sills sometimes project slightly, and evidences occur that the sides as well as the upper part of the window and doorway were made of adobe, now no longer in place. The jambs also were probably of clay, and the doors, made of slabs of stone, neatly fitted the orifices.

The prevailing storms in winter at Cliff Palace sweep up the canyon from the southwest, but there does not seem to have been a systematic effort to avoid the cold by placing doors and windows on the opposite side of the building; the openings, for instance, of the Speaker-chief's House face this direction and are open to storms of snow and rain. Many of the openings never had doors and windows, but were probably closed with sticks tied together, or with matting.[a] Certain windows were half closed, probably to temper the winter blasts. The sills of doors were commonly placed a foot or more above the floor;[b] transoms above the door opening and peepholes at the side are not common in Cliff Palace. In some cases a stepping-stone projects from the wall below the door opening to facilitate entrance; in others a foot hole is found in the same relative place.

As the jambs, sills, and lintels were built hard and fast in the mortar, evidently both door openings and windows were constructed when the corresponding wall was built. The jambs in some instances and the lintels in others are of split sticks, the surfaces of which are fibrous and were evidently not split by means of iron implements. There is evidence that the size of the door openings was sometimes reduced by a ridge of mortar which was arched above, as at Spruce-tree House, the intention being to make in this way a jamb to hold in place the stone door. There are no round windows of large size, but both doors and windows are quadrilateral in shape; the small circular openings in some of the walls may have served for lookouts.

FLOORS AND ROOFS

Not a single entire roof remained in Cliff Palace, and only one or two rooms retained remnants of rafters. It would seem, however, from the position of the holes in the walls into which the rafters

---

[a] Some of the doorways were filled with rude masonry; evidently the rooms were thus closed in some instances before the buildings were deserted.

[b] The placing of the sill at a level with the floor is a modern innovation at Walpi. The oldest houses still have it elevated, as in Cliff Palace. In some of the cliff-houses of the Navaho Monument sills and floor levels are continuous.

once extended that they were constructed like those of Spruce-tree House, a good example of which is shown in plate 9 of the report on that ruin. The floors seem to have been formed of clay hardened by tramping, but there is no evidence of paving with flat stones. The hardened adobe is sometimes laid on sticks without bark and stamped down. Although no instance of extensive rock cutting of the floor was observed in secular rooms, this is a common feature of kiva floors. Floors were generally level, but in some instances, when rock was encountered, the surface was raised in part above the other level. The majority of the floors had been dug into for buried specimens before the repair work was begun, but here and there fragments of floors were still intact, showing their former level. Banquettes or ledges around the walls are rare. In a few instances the unplastered roof of the cave served as the roof of the highest rooms.

FIREPLACES

Many fireplaces still remain in rooms, but the majority are found in convenient corners of the plazas.[a] The most common situation is in an angle formed by two walls, in which case the fire-pit is generally rimmed with a slightly elevated rounded ridge of adobe. In room 84 there is a fireplace in the middle of the floor. At one side of this depression there extends a supplementary groove in the floor, rimmed with stone, the use of which is not known. Although fireplaces are ordinarily half round, a square one occurs in the northwestern corner of room 81. All the fireplaces contained wood ashes, sometimes packed hard; but no cinders, large fragments of charcoal, or coal ashes were evident. The sides of the walls above the fireplaces are generally blackened with smoke.

The fire-holes of the kivas, being specially constructed, are different in shape from those in secular houses. While the cooking fire-pits are generally shallow, kiva fire-holes a foot deep are not exceptional, and several are much deeper. The fire was kindled in the kiva not so much for heating the room as for lighting it, there being no windows for that purpose. Certain kinds of fuel were probably prescribed, but logs were not burned in kivas on account of the heat. No evidences of smoke-hoods or chimneys have been found in any of the Cliff Palace rooms. The walls of many kivas showed blackening by soot or smoke.

LIVING ROOMS

It is difficult to distinguish rooms in which the inhabitants lived from others used by them for storage and other purposes, since most of their work, as cooking, pottery making, and like domestic

---

[a] Smoke on the walls of certain second and third stories shows that fireplaces were not restricted to the ground floor.

operations, was conducted either on the house-tops or in the plazas. Under living rooms are included the women's rooms,[a] or those in which centered the family life; and, in a general way, we may suppose the large rooms and those with banquettes were sleeping rooms. The popular misconception that the cliff-dwellers were of small stature has undoubtedly arisen from the diminutive size of all the secular rooms, but it must be remembered that the life of the cliff-dwellers was really an out-of-door one, the roof of the cave affording the necessary protection.

MILLING ROOMS

There are several rooms in Cliff Palace which appear to have been given up solely to the operation of grinding corn. The mills are box-like structures, constructed of slabs of stone set on edge, each containing a slanting stone called a metate, from which the mill is called by the Hopi the *metataki*, or " metate house." The following description of a metataki in pueblos seen by Castañeda in 1540 applies, in a general way, to the small milling troughs in Cliff Palace:

One room is appointed for culinary purposes, another for the grinding of corn; the latter is isolated [not so in Cliff Palace] and contains an oven and three stones [one, two, three, or four in Cliff Palace], cemented finely together. Three women sit [kneel] before these stones; the first crushes the corn, the second grinds it, and the third reduces it quite to a powder.

In grinding corn, which was generally the work of the girls or young women, the grinder knelt before the metataki and used a flat stone, which was rubbed back and forth on the metate. The corn meal thus ground fell into a squarish depression, made of smooth stones, at the lower end of the metate. Commonly the corners of this receptacle for the meal that had been ground were filled in with clay, and on each side of the metate were inserted fragments of pottery, which rounded the corners and made it easier to brush the meal into a heap. In room 92, where there are four metates, occupying almost the whole milling room, there are upright stones on the side of the wall, back of the place where the women knelt, against which they braced their feet.

Most of the grinding boxes were destroyed, but those in the Speaker-chief's house and others west of kiva V, especially the latter, were still in good condition, the metates being in place. Evidences of former metatakis were apparent in the floor of several other rooms, as in a room back of kiva K. It is evident from the number of metates found in Cliff Palace that several milling rooms, not now recognizable, formerly existed, and it is probable that every large clan had its

---

[a] Among the Hopi the oldest woman, as a clan representative, owns the living rooms, but kivas are the property of the men, the kiva chief of certain fraternities being the direct descendant of the clan chief of the ceremony when limited to his clan.

own milling room, with one or more metatakis, according to necessity. Although many metates without metatakis occur in Cliff Palace, that in itself is not evidence that they were moved from place to place by the inhabitants. These milling rooms were apparently roofed, low, and one-storied, possibly in some instances open on top, but generally had a small peephole or window for the entrance of light or for permitting the grinders to see passers-by.

GRANARIES

Under the general name of granaries are included storage rooms, some of which are situated below living rooms.[a] Here corn for consumption was stacked, and if we may follow Hopi customs in our interpretation of cliff-dwellers' habits, the people of Cliff Palace no doubt had a supply sufficient to prevent famine by tiding over a failure of crops for two or more years. Many of these chambers were without doorways or windows; they were not limited to storage of corn, but served for the preservation of any food products or valuable cult paraphernalia. Each clan no doubt observed more or less secrecy in the amount of corn it kept for future use, and on that account the storage rooms were ordinarily hidden from view.

The droppings of chipmunks and other rodents show that these commensals were numerous, and their presence made necessary the building of storage rooms in such manner that they would be proof against the ravages of such animals. The three cists constructed of stone slabs placed vertically, situated back of the Speaker-chief's House, sometimes called " eagle houses," were probably storage bins; in support of this hypothesis may be mentioned the fact that the cobs, tassels, and leaves of corn are said to have been abundant in them when Cliff Palace was first visited by white men.

Although eagle bones are found in the refuse in the unoccupied part of the cave back of the houses, their abundance does not necessarily prove that eagles were confined in them by the inhabitants of Cliff Palace. Perhaps the eagle nests in the canyon were owned by different clans and were visited yearly or whenever feathers were needed, and the dead eagles were probably buried ceremonially in these places, which therefore may be called eagle cemeteries, as among the Hopi.[b]

CREMATORIES

As is well known to students of the Southwest, the tribes of Indians dwelling along the lower Colorado river disposed of their dead by cremation, and evidences of burning the dead are found

[a] Genetically the room for storage of property was of earliest construction. This custom, which was necessary among agriculturists whose food supply was bulky, may have led to the choice of caves, natural or artificial, for habitation.

[b] See Property Rights in Eagles, *American Anthropologist,* vol. II, pp. 690–707, 1907.

among all the ruins along the Gila and Salt rivers in southern Arizona. The custom was also practiced in the San Pedro and Salt River valleys, and along other tributaries of the Gila river. Castañeda (1540) says that the inhabitants of Cibola, identified with Zuñi, burned their dead, but no indication of this practice is now found among existing Pueblos. The ancient Pueblo inhabitants of the Little Colorado, so far as known, did not burn their dead, and no record has been made of the practice among their descendants, the Hopi and Zuñi.

In his excellent work on the ruins of the Mesa Verde, Baron Nordenskiöld speaks of calcined human bones being found in a stone cist at Step House, and Mr. Wetherill is referred to as having observed evidence of cremation elsewhere among the Mesa Verde cliff-dwellings. There can be no doubt from the observations made in the refuse heaps at Cliff Palace that the inhabitants of this village not only burned their dead but there was a special room in the depths of the cave which was set aside for that purpose.[a] One of these rooms, situated at the northern end of the refuse heap, was excavated in the progress of the work and found to contain bushels of very fine phosphate ashes, mixed with fragments of bones, some of which are well enough preserved to enable their identification as human. Accompanying these calcined bones were various mortuary objects not unlike those occurring in graves where the dead were not cremated. The existence of great quantities of ashes, largely containing phosphates, apparently derived from the burned bones, forming much of the refuse, and the densely smoke-blackened roof of the cave above them, are interpreted to indicate that the dead were cremated in the cave back of the houses.

In addition to these burning places, or crematories, in the rear of the buildings of Cliff Palace, there is good evidence of the same practice on the mesa top. Here and there, especially in the neighborhood of the clearings where the cliff-dwellers formerly had their farms, are round stone inclosures, oftentimes several feet deep, in which occur great quantities of bone ashes, fragments of pottery, and some stone objects. The surface of the stones composing these inclosures shows the marks of intense fire, which, taken in connection with the existence of fragments of human bones more or less burned, indicate that the dead were cremated in these inclosures. It is not clear, however, that the dead were not interred before cremation, and there is reason for believing that the bodies were dried before they were committed to the flames. The mortuary offerings, especially pottery, seem to

---

[a] While only one place where bodies were burned was found in Cliff Palace, several such places were found on top of the mesa. Evidences of similar inclosures occur at Spruce-tree House and at Step House.

have been placed in the burning places after the heat had subsided, for beautiful jars showing no action of fire were found in some of these inclosures. The existence of cremation among the cliff-dwellers is offered as an explanation of the great scarcity of skeletons in their neighborhood. When it is remembered that Cliff Palace must have had a population of several hundred, judging from the number of the buildings, and was inhabited for several generations, it otherwise would be strange that so few skeletons were found. It would appear that the chiefs or the priestly class were buried either in the ground or in the floors of the rooms, which were afterward sealed, whereas the bodies of the poorer class, or the people generally, were cremated. The former existence of Pueblo peoples who buried their dead in the region between the Gila valley and Mesa Verde where the dead were cremated is a significant fact, but further observations are necessary before it can be interpreted. It may be that in ancient times all the sedentary tribes practiced cremation, and that the region in question was settled after this custom had been abandoned.

LEDGE ROOMS

In a shallow crevice in the roof of the cave on a higher level than the roofs of the tallest houses there is a long wall, the front of inclosures that may be called "ledge rooms." [a] Some of these rooms have plastered walls, others are roughly laid; the latter form one side of a court and served to shield those passing from one room to another. On this outer wall, about midway, there is painted in white an inverted terrace figure, which may represent a rain cloud. Attention should be called to the resemblance in form and position of this figure to that on an outside wall overlooking plaza C of Spruce-tree House. This series of ledge rooms was probably entered from the roof of a building in front, and the opening or doorway above room 66 served as such an entrance, according to several stockmen who visited Cliff Palace in earlier days.

ENUMERATION OF THE ROOMS IN CLIFF PALACE

SECULAR ROOMS

The rooms in Cliff Palace, now numbered from 1 to 94, include all those on the ground floor, but do not embrace the second, third, and fourth stories nor the elevated ledge rooms secluded in the crevices of the cave roof at a high level. Their classification by function

---

[a] This type of building is believed to be the oldest in those sections of the Southwest where cliff habitations occur.

already having been considered, a brief enumeration by form and other characters will be given.

Room 1, situated at the extreme southern end, presents no striking features except that one of its entrances is by stairs through the floor from kiva A. Its western and northern walls are of masonry; the remaining sides are formed by the vertical cliff.

The walls of room 2 are constructed of masonry on the northern, western, and southern sides; the eastern side is the cliff face. As the floor of this room is made of hardened clay laid on small sticks, it was at first supposed that a human burial was concealed beneath, but excavation showed no signs of an interment.

Room 3 (pl. 17) is a square inclosure between walls of other rooms. A portion of its floor is level with that of rooms 1 and 2, but a projecting rock forms an elevated bench on the eastern side. On the underside of this rock there are pictographs, apparently aboriginal, one of which has a well-known terrace form, recalling the outlines of a T-shaped doorway and the white figures on the outer wall of the ledge room above mentioned.

Room 4 is three stories high, without openings into adjoining rooms or exterior entrances. Its western corner is rounded below and angular above.

Room 5 was apparently two stories high, with a fireplace in its southeastern corner. The foundation rests on a large rock. The arrangement of post holes in the south and west walls of this dwelling is exceptional, and their purpose enigmatical. There is a passage from room 5 to the neighboring plaza, which is occupied by kiva D.

Room 6 is a small rectangular chamber, about 2 feet square and 7 feet high; it has an entrance on the western side into room 7, and, as it utilizes the walls of the adjacent rooms, it was doubtless built subsequent to them. Evidences of rebuilding or secondary construction of walls on old foundations are so numerous in this section of the ruin that this may be the oldest part of Cliff Palace.

Rooms 7, 8, and 9 are outside rooms, the western walls of which are more or less broken, while the front is entirely destroyed. It appears that their connected roofs once formed a terrace overlooking kiva D on the west. There are doorways in walls of one of these rooms, but entrance may have been gained by means of hatchways. It was approached from plaza B by the aid of ladders or stone steps.

Room 11, which may be called the square tower, is the only four-story building standing in Cliff Palace, its walls reaching from the floor to the roof of the cave. When work began on this building the whole northwestern angle had fallen, and the remaining walls were tottering. To prevent total destruction, the entire corner was built up from a foundation laid on the floor level of the neighboring kiva. A small entrance to the ground floor, or the lowest of the four rooms, is from a banquette (10) on the western side, where there is a passageway from this lower story of room 11 to room 12, situated in its rear. Room 12 has a good floor, and room 11 a fireplace in the southwestern corner of the lowest room of the square tower. Almost all the beams of the higher rooms of this tower had been taken out, leaving nothing but the holes in the walls to indicate the former existence of floors. The beams now connecting the walls were placed there by our workmen to serve as staging and for tying the sides together. The second and third stories of the square tower are also without floors. Their inner walls are plastered a reddish color, in places whitewashed, and the third wall is decorated with interesting paintings. In the western wall of the second story was a small window, and portions of a large T-shaped doorway still show on the northern wall of the third story. Split sticks support the section of wall from the top of this doorway to the roof of the cave. From the arrangement of its rear walls it would appear that the whole of this tower was built subsequently to the rooms back of it, which extend on each side, north and south. The repair of a doorway of the northern wall was difficult, the foundation walls of the eastern and northern corners of the tower being slabs of stone set on edge, quite inadequate to support the lofty wall above. This insufficient foundation leads to the belief that when the base of the square tower was constructed there was no thought of erecting upon it the four stories that we now find. (Pl. 12, 13a, 14a.)

Some of the rooms of the square tower bear evidence of having been living rooms, and possibly the approaches to the upper chambers were by ladders from the outside; otherwise the T-shaped doorway on the northern side, above the painted room, remains unexplained.

Room 12, situated east of the square tower, has no characteristic features, being more a passageway than a room, opening at one end into room 13 and connecting with kiva D at the other end.

Room 13 likewise presents no distinctive features; its rear wall is considerably blackened by smoke, and it has a large square window opening into room 12.

A large part of the front walls of rooms 14, 16, and 24 has fallen, having been destroyed by falling water. To obviate future destruction, the southwestern corner of room 16 was repaired with cement, thus preventing further harm from dripping water. Rooms 16 and 24 evidently formed a front terrace, perhaps one story high, their rear wall being the front wall of rooms 17 and 18.

Rooms 17 and 18 are of two stories; both are square. The upper part of its walls shows that a portion of room 18 was formerly one story high and that the walls were erected before those of room 17. A coping of masonry around three walls is a feature of room 18, the construction of which is superior to that of room 17. This room has a large front window and two smaller openings higher up in the second story of the western wall. The combined front walls of rooms 17 and 18 may be ranked among the finest examples of masonry in Cliff Palace. The large embrasures made in this wall by vandals were repaired.

Rooms 19 and 20 also present fine examples of masonry and were evidently constructed before rooms 21, 22, and 23. The inner walls of room 19 were plastered; the outer wall was left rough. Room 20 shows crude masonry; its rear wall is the vertical cliff, and the inner surfaces of the three remaining walls of the upper story were plastered, and painted with yellow sand or pigment. Apparently the lower room was used as a granary, having no entrance, except possibly through a hatchway in its roof, which forms the floor of the room above. The presence of sticks projecting from the walls of this room adds weight to the conclusion that it was used for storage. There is no indication of a fireplace.

Room 22 has a stepping-stone, which may have facilitated entrance, projecting from the wall under an opening that probably served as a doorway.

Room 23 has a fireplace in one corner, and rooms 25, 26, and 27, which are situated in a row, have for their rear wall the vertical face of the cliff. Although these rooms are only one story high, the roof of the cave slopes down low enough in the rear to form their roofs. The outer walls were plastered, and each room was entered by a separate doorway. Although their side walls were somewhat destroyed, they appear not to have been intercommunicating. It is, in fact, rare to find a doorway from one room into another on the same level, or suites of rooms communicating with one another, but chambers one above another are generally provided with hatchways.

Room 28 is a two-story structure of excellent masonry, with an entrance on its southern side and a window frame of stone. Its second story formerly opened on the western side into room 29. Not much now remains of the plastering that once covered the inner walls of room 28, but the interior walls of room 29 still show well-preserved plaster. Although the latter room has excellent masonry, its southern wall, or that facing kiva J, is entirely destroyed. The floor was so well preserved that but little work was required to put it in good condition.

Rooms 30 to 33 are represented almost entirely by the side walls, the front walls being more or less destroyed. Their floors lie on the same level as those of the second terrace, and their roofs may have been continuous with the third terrace. There is indication of a room (unnumbered) in the southwestern corner of plaza J, and another, too mutilated to be described, on the second terrace below it.

Room 34 is irregularly rectangular in shape; its floor is on the level of the roof of kiva H. It has good masonry and a smoothed stone sill with a groove cut in the upper surface for the slab that formed the door. Its interior walls show evidences of plastering.

Room 35, situated on the same level as the kiva roof, has no window, but there is an opening directly into kiva H. Its roof is a continuation of that of the kiva, and has the old rafters, some still in place, supporting a few of the flat stones which formed the upper walls. As this chamber opens directly into the kiva, we may regard it as a repository for kiva paraphernalia;[a] the Hopi designate a similar chamber *Katcinakihu*, "Katcina house." On the roof of this room the writer set in place a smooth, ovoid stone with flat base, artificially worked. Possibly this stone was formerly used as an idol.

In Hano, a pueblo on the East mesa of the Hopi, masks are kept in a special room back of a living room, a custom common to all the Hopi. There is no evidence that the Cliff Palace people performed masked dances.

The most picturesque building of Cliff Palace is the round tower, room 36, perched on a high rock overlooking kivas G and H. From it the observer may have a fine view of the entire ruin and the canyon, especially the view down the latter, which is unsurpassed. This tower is not unlike other towers in the San Juan and Mesa Verde regions, one of the most perfect of which is that in Navaho canyon, repeatedly figured. This prominent tower is built of worked stones laid in reddish mortar, and apparently was plastered both inside and outside. It is two stories high, but is without a floor in the upper story, or a roof. The theory in certain quarters that this round tower formerly extended to the roof of the cave is not accepted by the author, who believes that it was formerly only a few feet higher than at present. The break in the upper wall adds much to its picturesque character, which is likewise increased by its association with neighboring buildings. The round tower has a doorway in its lower story, and above is another smaller opening, possibly a window. Several small peepholes are present on the western side. The sides of this structure are symmetrical, its walls slanting gradually inward from the base upward, and its vertical lines curving slightly on the western side. (Pl. 4*a*, 11.)

Room 37 is a well-preserved room with a metataki, or grinding bin, in the middle.

While rooms 38 and 39 appear to be living rooms, they present no special peculiarities. The northern wall of room 39 was wholly un-

---

[a] The Mongkiva at Walpi has such a chamber which is closed by a door and is opened only when paraphernalia for certain ceremonies are desired. In the Warrior House at Walpi there is a similar chamber, ordinarily closely sealed, in which the fetishes of the Warrior Society are kept. Masked dancers among the Pueblos are called Katcinas, and the masks they wear would naturally be kept in a house (*kihu*) called "Katcinakihu."

dermined and tottering when the work of repair was commenced, so that its foundations had to be built up from the floor of kiva M. To make this difficult repair work effective it was necessary to enlarge the base of the wall, making the side of kiva M curve slightly inward and thereby insuring a good foundation.

The walls of rooms 41 and 42 are well preserved; the top of the cave served as the roof. These rooms were entered from the plaza containing kiva M. In room 42 a stepping-stone is set in the outer wall below the doorway, the object being to facilitate entrance. It is said that this room, the roof of which shows signs of smoke, was occupied by campers while engaged in rifling the ruin of its contents.

The cluster of rooms numbered 43 to 45 have well-constructed walls, but they have been considerably mutilated. Pegs from which, no doubt, objects were formerly hung, project from the smoothly plastered interior walls of one of these rooms.

Rooms 47 and 48 show the holes of floor joists, so placed as to indicate two stories. These rooms form the southern side of the court, which extends from the main plaza of the settlement to the round rooms at the northern extremity. In front of room 50 there is a low platform from which one steps into the room through an entrance situated about midway of its length.

Room 51 has a very well preserved fireplace in the northwestern corner and a doorway about midway in the northern wall. Its well-plastered walls show impressions of the hands and fingers of the plasterers.

The eastern side of the " street "[a] is bordered by rooms 60 to 63, inclusive, which open into it. In the wall of the last room (61) to the south there is a small peephole that enabled the owners to see from within the room anyone entering the street from the court. Room 59, probably the largest angular room in Cliff Palace, is without an entrance. Its high walls form a part of the northern and eastern ends of the court and almost the whole western side of the street. A large embrasure in its southern wall had been repaired by the ancient masons before Cliff Palace was deserted. North of room 59 remains of the foundations of rooms (not numbered on the plan) were found, and it may be possible that at this point there was a small open space, without a kiva; if so, it would have been exceptional in Cliff Palace.

Rooms 66 and 68 are round rooms, not kivas, although possibly ceremonial in character. From the roof of room 66, the walls of which are now lower than formerly, it was possible to pass on a level into one of the series of ledge rooms previously described. The floor of room 68 is exceptional in being lower than that of the cave outside,

---

[a] A passage or inclosure surrounded by high walls is called *kisombi* by the **Hopi**.

so that on entering it one descends by a step or two. Room 67 appears to have been more a passageway (*kisombi*) than a room, a step from it leading down to the level of the triangular plaza in front of the Speaker-chief's House, south of room 70.

Room 70 is a milling room, with two well-preserved metatakis in one corner, each with a set of metates. In the wall above these meal- ing troughs there is a small window through which the women en- gaged in grinding corn could see the passers through the court east of this room. The opposite corner is occupied by a fireplace, and the adjacent wall is pierced by a doorway with elevated threshold, through which one passed from the milling room to the broad Speaker-chief's platform south of rooms 71 and 72.

The inclosed space west of rooms 71 and 73 is separated from the rear of the cave by a high wall which shuts off entrance on this side. The series of rooms numbered 71 to 74, and the two rooms west of these, form, with the banquette and the neighboring plaza, what is here arbitrarily designated the Speaker-chief's House, the walls of which consist of some of the finest masonry in Cliff Palace. It is protected on the western side by a high, well-plastered wall extending southward·from the corner of room 72, so placed as to shield the plaza from storms from this side. The banquette south of rooms 72 and 73 is also finely plastered, and is approached from the plaza by a single step. This banquette probably was designed for the use of the Speaker-chief, but a similar structure on the eastern side of the plaza quarter served another purpose.

The masonry, the doors and windows, and other structural features of the Speaker-chief's House are the best in Cliff Palace. Lintels, jambs, and door and window sills are of smooth-dressed stones and project beyond the wall. The rear rooms of this cluster extend to the roof of the cave, being three stories high, while those in front are two stories in height. The line of holes shown in plate 15 indi- cates the former position of rafters, but all signs of woodwork have disappeared from this section of the ruin.

On the western side of the Speaker-chief's House are two rooms, 79 and 80, likewise well built. The former has a banquette extending across the eastern side, and the latter is triangular in shape, with the exterior side rounded. The foundations of these rooms rest upon a large rock that has settled and cracked, the crack extending vertically into the walls, showing that it has developed since the wall was constructed.

The inclosures 76 to 78, extending to the cave roof, are more like granaries for the storage of corn. They are built of flat stone slabs placed on edge, and rest on bowlders that have fallen from the cave roof, which is here lower than in the middle part of the cavern. Of these inclosures, 78 is the best preserved, all holes in its angles being skillfully closed with adobe mortar, so that even now if the door were replaced it would be almost rat proof. The door opening is square, and is situated at the western side. There is no adequate evidence that these rooms served as turkey houses, as some have interpreted them.

The rear walls of rooms 89 and 90 are well preserved, but those in front have been completely destroyed. The former has a banquette like that of the Speaker-chief's House. The walls of rooms situated north and east of kiva U, now reduced in height, formerly extended to the roof of the cave, which is here somewhat lower than in the middle of the cavern. The existence of these former walls is indicated by light bands on the smoke-covered surface of the cave roof, and fragments of clay still adhering to the side of the cliff show that the walls here were two and three stories high.

In rooms 84, 85, and 86 the builder took advantage of the cliff for rear walls. The middle of the floor of 84 has a depression lined with vertical slabs of stone, evidently a fireplace, as it contained a quantity of wood ashes. In the floor on the eastern side of this fireplace there is a short trench also lined with stone and containing wood ashes, the relation of which to the other inclosure is unknown. It appears that this exceptional structure was not used in the same way as the fireplaces so constantly met with in other rooms, but that it might have been used for baking paper-bread, called *piki* by the Hopi. In a corner of room 91 there is another depression, half under the floor, covered with a flat stone, that appears quite likely to have been used for this purpose. Unlike the fireplaces sunken in the floor, the one in room 84 is partially or wholly above the floor, its confining stones being several inches above the floor level.

Room 92 is the best example of a milling room in Cliff Palace. It has four grinding bins, or metatakis, arranged side by side, with all the parts entire and in working condition. When excavation was begun in this part of the ruin these structures were wholly concealed under fallen rocks. As streams of water from a vertical cleft in the cliff poured down upon them after exposure during periods of rain, it was necessary to construct a roof to protect them.[a] The discovery of this and of other grinding rooms shows that the cliff-house metatakis are the same in structure as those in the Hopi pueblos. In an inclosure south of these metatakis was found a granary. Fragments of walls projecting from the cliff west of room 93 show the former existence of rooms in this section, but as their front walls have been obliterated by the downpour of water their form is obscure.

---

[a] On the top of the rock that forms the foundation of the walls of these rooms, and south of them, are hollows or grooves where the metates were ground, and shallow pits used in some prehistoric game. There are similar pits in some of the kiva floors.

KIVAS

There are in Cliff Palace 23 ceremonial rooms that may be called kivas.[a] These consist of two types: (1) generally circular or cylindrical subterranean rooms, with pilasters to support the roof, and with fireplace, deflector, and ventilator. (2) Circular or rectangular rooms with rounded corners, without pilasters, fireplace, or deflector. In the first group may be placed provisionally a subtype (kiva M, for example), without pilasters but with a single large banquette. As this subtype is the dominant one in the western part of the San Juan drainage, it may be necessary later to regard it as a type. As a rule rooms of the second type are not subterranean, but are commonly surrounded by high walls, being entered by a doorway at one side. There are 20 rooms pertaining to the first type and three to the second type in Cliff Palace.[b]

The majority of the kivas are situated in front of the secular buildings, but several are in the rear of the cave, with high rooms in front of them. The largest cluster of kivas on the cave floor lies in the so-called plaza quarter, which takes its name from the open space occupied by the kivas in that section. The rooms on the terraces, especially those near the southern end of the ruin, were covered with fallen rocks and other débris when the excavation and repair work began. The walls of most of the kivas, whether in front or in the rear, were greatly dilapidated and in all instances it was necessary to rebuild them to the level of the plazas in which the kivas are situated.

Following comparisons with modern pueblos, there is every reason to suppose that the kivas preserve the oldest types of buildings of the cliff-dweller culture, and it is believed that the form of these archaic structures is a survival of antecedent conditions. They belonged to the men of different clans, as in a measure is the case among the Hopi at the present day, with whom every kiva is spoken of as that of a certain man who is a clan chief. The male and female members of every Hopi clan have affiliation with certain kivas (a survival of archaic conditions), and in certain clan gatherings, as the dramatic exhibition which occurs in March, the celebration takes place in their respective kivas.

---

[a] The word kiva, now universally employed in place of the Spanish designation "estufa" to designate a ceremonial room of the Pueblos, is derived from the Hopi language. The designation is archaic, the element ki being both Pima and Hopi for "house." It has been sought to connect this word with a part of the human body, and esoterically the kiva represents one of the underworlds or womb of the earth from which the races of man were born. It is highly appropriate that ancient ceremonies should take place in a kiva, the symbolic representation of an underworld, for many of the ceremonies are said to have been practiced while man still lived within the Earth Mother. The word kiva is restricted to subterranean chambers, rectangular or circular, in which secret ceremonies are or were held, and the term kihu is suggested for ceremonial rooms above ground. The five kivas at Walpi are examples of the true kiva, while the Flute chamber may be called a kihu.

[b] The so-called "warrior room" in Spruce-tree House belongs to the second type.

As the kiva is the men's room, and as religious exercises are largely controlled by men, such ceremonies occur in kivas, which are practically the ceremonial rooms.[a]

KIVAS OF THE FIRST TYPE

All kivas of the first type are constructed on the same general plan, the different parts being somewhat modified by surrounding conditions. While their general form is circular or cylindrical, some are square with rounded angles, others oblong, and others more or less heart-shaped. Their diameter and height vary according to circumstances, but this type is always subterranean when possible, even though excavation in the rock may be necessary.

The walls of the kivas are sometimes double, and the masonry is generally well constructed. The walls show evidences of plastering, which is decorated in some instances with paintings or incised figures. The number of pilasters is commonly 6, but 4 and 8 are also evident; rarely, as in kiva M (the subtype), all are missing. Between these pilasters are the so-called banquettes, one of which is usually larger than the others. The banquettes are generally built 3 or 4 feet in height, consequently they could scarcely have been intended for seats.

The pilasters are commonly rectangular, sometimes square, the size being about uniform from base upward. In rare instances a pilaster has a cubby-hole[b] in one side. Where circumstances require the ventilator penetrates the rear portion of the pilaster, but the flue never enters the side of the kiva under a pilaster.

The pilasters, which are almost universal in kivas of the first type, as has been shown in the description and illustrations of the eight kivas of Spruce-tree House, served as supports for the roof beams. These rafters of pine rested upon and served to support other logs laid one over another, so that finally the roof opening was covered. Across the middle of the walls, at the top, two long parallel logs were placed, in order to add stability to the roof structure. These beams were set far enough apart to allow a hatch midway between their ends, which served the purpose of an entrance and also permitted the escape of smoke from the fire directly below.

Over the framework of logs were laid small sticks, filling the interstices, and above these was spread a layer of cedar bark; the whole was then covered with clay, thus bringing the upper surface of the roof to the level of the adjacent plaza. Whether the kiva walls projected above the plaza and roof level is unknown, but possi-

---

[a] In certain ceremonies of Hopi women's societies the kiva has also come to be a meeting place for these sororities and where they erect their altars.

[b] These small holes, generally square, are usually found in the wall below the banquette.

bly they did, and there may have been a slight elevation of the hatchway, as in the Hopi kivas. It is commonly believed that the kiva roof was level with the surrounding plaza and that the entrance was through a hatchway, but no depression or other sign of a ladder or of its resting place on the kiva floor has yet been found in any of the Mesa Verde ruins.

The floors of the kivas are commonly of hardened adobe; unlike those of the Hopi kivas they are never paved with stones, but the natural rock often serves for that purpose. It is not rare to find the surface of solid rock that forms the kiva floor cut down a few feet to a lower level. Although generally smooth, when the floor is the natural rock there are sometimes found in it small, cup-like, artificial depressions similar to those in the horizontal surfaces of the cliff or in slabs of detached rock.

The fire-pit, which is found in all kivas of the first type,[a] is a circular depression situated slightly to one side of the middle of the room. While generally lined with adobe, slabs of stone sometimes form its border, and it is also to be noted that one or two of these small stones sometimes project above the floor level. The fire-hole is sometimes deep, and is generally filled with wood ashes, indicating long use.

Every kiva of the first type has a lateral passageway for the admission of air, opening into the chamber on the floor level, generally under the large banquette. This passage, or tunnel, here designated a flue, communicates either directly with the outside or turns upward at a right angle and forms a small vertical ventilator which opens at the level of the plaza. Between the entrance into the flue from the kiva and the fire-hole there rises from the floor a device called the deflector (sometimes called an altar), the object of which was to prevent flames and smoke being drawn into the ventilator, or to evenly circulate the inflowing fresh air in the chamber. This deflector may be (1) a low stone wall, free on both ends; (2) a curved wall connected with the kiva wall on each side with orifices to allow the passage of air; (3) a stone slab in the kiva floor; (4) a bank, free at each end, supported by upright stakes between which are woven twigs, the whole being plastered with clay.[b]

The supposed functions of the flue, the vertical passage, and the ventilator have been discussed by several archeologists. The uses to which the flue has been ascribed are as follows: (1) a chimney, (2) a

---

[a] The fire in these rooms was more for light than for heat, for when roofed a large fire would have produced so much smoke and heat that the occupants would be driven out. The character of the ashes indicates that logs were not used as firewood, but that the prescribed kiva fuel was, as at Walpi, small twigs or brush. No evidence of lamps has been found in cliff-dwellings, the lamp-shaped pottery objects having been used for purposes other than illumination.

[b] Cosmos Mindeleff quotes from Nordenskiöld a description of a Mesa Verde kiva, the deflector of which was made in the same way.

ceremonial opening, (3) an entrance, (4) a ventilator. There is no sign of smoke on the interior of the vertical passage, which, being too small to admit a person, would seem to prove the first and third theories untenable. In the Navaho National Monument, where there are square rooms, or *kihus*, with banks similar to the deflectors of the circular kivas, a door takes the place of the flue and the vertical passage, and affords the only means for admitting fresh air to the room. Although it may have originated as a simple entrance to the room, it became so modified that it could no longer have served that purpose, ceremonially or otherwise.

The position of the entrance to the Cliff Palace kiva is yet to be definitely determined. Analogy, together with the structure of the roof, would indicate that it was by means of a hatchway, but no remains of a ladder were found, and no indication in the floor where a ladder formerly rested is visible. It may be that the large banquette indicates the position of the hatchway.[a]

The subterranean passageway under the flue and beneath the floor of kiva V should not be overlooked in a study of the origin and function of the ventilator. This structure is without apparent connection with the ventilator, and yet it is so carefully constructed under it that it may have had some relation, a knowledge of which will eventually enlighten us regarding the meaning of both structures.

The kivas of the Mesa Verde are much smaller than those of Walpi and other Hopi pueblos, one of them being barely 9 feet in diameter and the largest measuring not more than 19 feet, whereas the chief kiva at Walpi is 25 feet long by 15 feet wide. Evidently kivas of such diminutive size as those found at Cliff Palace could accommodate only a few at a time, and it is probable that they were not occupied by fraternities of priests but by a few chiefs; indeed, the religious fraternity, as we understand its composition in modern pueblos, had in all probability not yet been developed. Nevertheless the smallest kiva in Cliff Palace is as large as the room in Walpi in which the Sun priests, mainly of one clan, celebrate their rites.

KIVA A

Kiva A (pl. 17) is the most southerly kiva of Cliff Palace, the first of the series excavated in the talus, its roof having been on the level of the cave floor, or the fourth terrace. The walls of this kiva required little repair. Its height from the floor to the top of the walls is 8 feet 6 inches, and from the floor to the top of the pilasters 7 feet; the height of the banquette is 3 feet 6 inches. The interior diameter is 11 feet. There are six pilasters, with an average breadth of 20 inches; the distance between them averages 4 feet 6 inches.

---

[a] On this supposition the large banquette may have been the forerunner of the spectator's section in the modern rectangular Hopi kivas, of which it is a modification.

The opening into the ventilator is situated in the southwestern wall; its height is 2 feet 4 inches, the breadth, at the base, 14 inches, contracted to 11 inches at the top. The deflector, which is broken, is a thin slab of stone. The distance from the flue opening to the deflector is 2 feet 6 inches, and from the deflector to the round fire-hole 8 inches. The diameter of the fire-hole is 1 foot 8 inches, its depth 2 feet. Its western side is lined with small stones set on edge.

There were possibly 4 niches in the side wall of the banquette, 3 of them on the east, measuring respectively 16 by 20 by 12 inches, 9 by 9 by 12 inches, and 3 by 3 by 5 inches, and the remaining one situated north by east from the middle of the kiva and measuring 6 by 4 by 8 inches.[a]

There is a subterranean passageway (pl. 17, b), 6 feet 6 inches long, from this kiva into room 1, and also a tunnel (pl. 17, a), 6 feet in length, between kivas A and B. The former has stone steps and rises above the banquette; its width averages 18 inches.

KIVA B

Kiva B adjoins kiva A, and is the second of the terraced rooms, its roof being originally on the same level as the former. It is circular in shape, and the height from the floor to the top of the room is 9 feet 6 inches. The height of the top of the pilasters from the floor is 7 feet, and that of the banquette 3 feet 6 inches.

The inner diameter of the kiva is 13 feet 6 inches. There are 6 pilasters, averaging 2 feet in width. The position of the ventilator opening is south by west; its depth 4 feet, and height 2 feet 6 inches. The breadth of this opening at the top (it narrows somewhat at the base) is 18 inches.

The deflector[b] is a slab of stone about 3 feet 10 inches wide. The distance from the deflector to the kiva wall is 2 feet 6 inches, and from the deflector to the fire-hole 14 inches. The diameter of the fire-hole measures 2 feet, and its depth 9 inches. The distance from the ceremonial opening, or sipapû, to the fire-hole is 4 feet. The diameter of the sipapû is 4 inches and its depth the same. There are 5 niches in the kiva wall.

The masonry of this kiva is fairly good, its western wall naturally being the most destroyed. The banquette over the tunnel into kiva A is broader than any of the others. On the eastern side the kiva walls are apparently double.

---

[a] The measurements of the kivas here given were determined by Mr. R. G. Fuller, who served as voluntary assistant during the summer.

[b] With the exception of that in kiva Q there has not been found in any deflector a large stone ("fire stone") forming the cap or top. In deflectors formed of a slab of stone such a "fire stone" on top would be impossible.

KIVA C

This kiva is circular; it measures 13 feet in diameter, and 5 feet 6 inches from the floor to the top of the pilasters. The height of the banquette is 3 feet. The number of pilasters is 6; their average breadth is 2 feet.

The deflector is a stone wall laid in mortar; its width is 3 feet 6 inches; the thickness, 8 inches. From the flue to the deflector is 2 feet 4 inches, and from the same to the fire-hole, 8 inches. The diameter of the fire-hole is 2 feet, its depth 1 foot. The sipapû is 2 feet from the fire-hole; it is 6 inches deep and 4 inches in diameter.

The masonry of this kiva was in very poor condition, most of the upper part being wholly broken down. There are 4 niches in the walls. The surface is thickly plastered and shows a deposit of smoke. The pilasters are of uniform size. The deep banquette is situated above the flue back of the deflector.

KIVA D

Kiva D is square, with rounded corners; it is 13 feet in diameter; its walls are 10 feet high and measure 7 feet from the floor to the top of the pilasters. The height of the banquette is 4 feet. The number of pilasters is 6; their average distance apart is 4 feet 6 inches, and their width 2 feet. The eastern wall of this kiva is the side of the cave, and the whole was inclosed by high walls. On the southern side of the kiva is a passageway. The walls of the kiva and the cave roof above it are blackened with smoke. There are two deep banquettes.

The flue opens in the western wall of the kiva; its height is 2 feet, and its width at the top is 13 inches. The distance from the flue to the deflector is 2 feet 6 inches; from the deflector to the fire-hole, 13 inches. The diameter of the fire-hole is 2 feet and its depth 1 foot. The distance from the fire-hole to the sipapû is 2 feet 2 inches; the diameter of the latter is 3 inches. This kiva has 5 finely made rectangular niches in the walls. The walls are well plastered and were painted yellow. Wherever the masonry is visible it is found inferior to none except possibly that of kiva Q.[a]

KIVA E

Kiva E is square, with rounded corners; it measures 11 feet 6 inches in diameter, and is 9 feet 10 inches high. The elevation of the banquette is 4 feet, and of the pilasters 7 feet. The number of pilasters is 6. The flue opens on the western side.

The deflector consists of a wall of stone, 2 feet high; its width is 3 feet 6 inches, the thickness 9 inches. The distance from the deflector

---

[a] This kiva, which is one of the best in Cliff Palace, is illustrated by Nordenskiöld.

to the flue is 1 foot 10 inches, and from the fire-hole 3 inches. There are 4 mural niches. As the projecting rock on the eastern side interfered with the symmetry of this kiva, when constructed it was necessary to peck the rock away 8 inches deep over an area 10 feet square, thus exhibiting, next to the floor of kiva V, the most extensive piece of kiva stone-cutting in Cliff Palace. Although this kiva was generally in a fair state of preservation, it was necessary to rebuild much of the eastern wall.

The fire-hole of this kiva is lined with a rude jar set with adobe mortar. No sipapû was discovered in the floor. Kiva E is one of the few kivas in Cliff Palace surrounded by the walls of rooms. As it is situated in the rear of the cave, projecting walls of the cliff were necessarily cut away to a considerable extent in order to obtain the form of room desired on the eastern side. This side of the kiva is blackened by smoke antedating the construction of the room. There is abundant evidence in this portion of the ruin of secondary construction of buildings on the same site. Several walls built upon others show that some rooms may have been abandoned and new ones added, an indication that this portion of the ruin is very old, perhaps having the oldest walls still standing.

KIVA F

Kiva F, situated on a lower terrace than the kivas already described, is square, with rounded corners, and is 9 feet high. The height of the pilasters is 6 feet 10 inches, and the top of the banquette is 4 feet 1 inch above the floor. The diameter of the kiva is 13 feet. There are 6 pilasters; the distance between them averages 5 feet; their average width is 2 feet 4 inches. The deflector, a wall of masonry, is 3 feet wide and averages 9 inches in thickness.

The deflector is 2 feet from the flue and 18 inches from the fire-hole, which is 2 feet in diameter and the same in depth. The distance from the fire-hole to the sipapû is 2 feet 4 inches. The diameter of the sipapû is 2½ inches, and its depth 5 inches.

There are 3 mural niches, similar to those previously described. The roof of this kiva was of the same level as the floors of rooms 16 and 24, the roofs of which overlooked the kiva situated in the terrace below.

The walls of this kiva are black with smoke. The room is surrounded by a second wall, the interval between which and that of the kiva is filled with rubble.

KIVA G

This kiva may be called " heartshaped." Its height from the floor to the top of the roof is 9 feet, and it measures 6 feet from the floor to the top of the pilasters. The banquette is 4 feet high, and the interior diameter of the kiva is 12 feet. The numbers of pilasters is 6; their average breadth is a little more than 2 feet, and the intervals between them averages 3 feet 6 inches.

The deflector is a stone slab 3 feet wide and 2 feet high. The distance from the flue to the deflector is 2 feet; from the deflector to the fire-hole 11 inches. The diameter of the fire-hole is 2 feet, its depth 18 inches. The sipapû is 2 feet 8 inches from the fire-hole; its diameter is 2 inches, and its depth 4 inches. There are 4 mural niches.

This kiva is situated in the terrace below that last mentioned, that is, in the second terrace, and was wholly buried when excavations began. The roofs of rooms 30 and 31 overlooked this kiva, their floors being on the same level as the kiva roof.

KIVA H

Kiva H (pl. 18) measures 8 feet from the floor to the top of the wall, and 6 feet from the floor to the top of the pilasters. The height of the banquette is 4 feet 6 inches. The diameter of the kiva is 11 feet 6 inches.

The deflector is a curved stone wall joining the kiva wall on each side of the flue.[a] It is built of stone, 7 feet 6 inches high, 10 inches wide, and 20 inches high. The deflector is 1 foot 6 inches from the flue and 15 inches from the fire-hole. The diameter of the fire-hole is 2 feet and its depth 1 foot.

The sipapû is situated 2 feet from the fire-hole· it is 3 inches in diameter and 4 inches deep.

There are 2 mural niches. Exceptional features of this kiva are the curved deflector and the opening into a small room at the northwestern corner. Instead of extending straight from the kiva to the vertical ventilator, the flue turns at a right angle midway in its course. The ventilator is built at one corner of the kiva wall. As this kiva lies deep below the base of the round tower, a fine view of these several characteristics may be obtained from that point.

KIVA I

When work began there was no indication of the walls of this kiva, except a fragment of one which at first was supposed to belong to a small secular room. The kiva had been filled with débris by those who had dug into the upper rooms, and a large hole[b] was broken through the high western wall of kiva L, through which to throw débris. The removal of this accumulation was a work of

---

[a] A similar deflector is recorded by Mr. Morley as existing in the Cannonball ruin, and is figured by Nordenskiöld from the Mesa Verde.

[b] This entrance in the wall appears in all photographs of this portion of Cliff Palace.

considerable magnitude, and the repair of the kiva wall was very difficult, as it was necessary to reconstruct the foundations that had been blasted away to make the opening above mentioned.

When this débris was removed and the floor of the kiva was reached, it was found that its walls were much disintegrated, the component stones having practically turned into sand, necessitating the construction of buttresses to support them. The dimensions of kiva I are as follows: The height of the top of the wall from the floor is 8 feet, and that of the pilasters 6 feet 8 inches. The banquette rises 3 feet 8 inches above the floor. The interior diameter of the kiva is 10 feet 10 inches. The number of pedestals is 4, averaging 4 feet in height.

The flue is situated at the southwestern side. The distance from the flue to the deflector is 21 inches; from the deflector to the fire-hole, 2 inches. There are two mural niches, one at the northeast measuring 13 by 11 by 8 inches, and one at the southeast measuring 13 by 11 by 7 inches. A dado, painted red, surrounded the kiva, the color being most conspicuous, because best protected, in the mural niches, half of which are above, half below the upper margin of the dado. On this margin are traceable triangular figures like those on the painted wall of room 11.

On the level of what was formerly the roof of this kiva was set into the roof a vase covered with a flat stone and containing desiccated bodies of lizards.[a]

KIVA J

Kiva J is round; it is 14 feet in diameter and measures 8 feet 4 inches from the floor to the top of the wall. The height from the floor to the top of one of the pilasters is 5 feet 10 inches. The banquette is 3 feet 2 inches high. The deep banquette, as is usually the case, is above the flue, which opens in the southwestern wall. The number of pedestals is 6; their average breadth is 2 feet. The deflector consists of a stone wall rising 20 inches above the kiva floor. There are 7 mural niches. The kiva walls were thickly plastered with adobe, and show the action of smoke.[b]

The open space east of the kiva, formerly continuous with its roof, is somewhat larger than is usually the case, making this the largest plaza in Cliff Palace, except that of the plaza quarter. There are remnants of rooms southwest of the kiva.

---

[a] For a note on a similar vase and its use, see remarks on kiva S. It is probable that these dried lizards were regarded by the Cliff Palace priests as very potent " medicine."

[b] From all appearances the kivas were plastered from time to time after the walls had become blackened.

KIVA K

Kiva K[a] is round in form, and its height from the floor to the roof is 7 feet. The height of the pilasters is 5 feet, and that of the banquette 3 feet. The diameter of the kiva is 9 feet 6 inches. The pilasters are 5 in number, and average about 20 inches in width. The deflector of this kiva is exceptional, being the only known instance where this structure is constructed of upright stakes bound with twigs or cedar bark and plastered with adobe.[b] The distance from the flue to the deflector is 18 inches, and from the deflector to the fire-hole, 8 inches. The diameter of the fire-hole is 20 inches, the depth 8 inches. The walls of this smallest of the kivas are formed partly of masonry, but in places the chamber is excavated out of solid rock, the ancient builders having pecked away projections in order to produce the desired form.

The marks of smoke are clearly visible, especially on the flue; and on the surface of the eastern side are scratched several figures representing birds and other animals. Eyelets of osiers set in the wall are also exceptional, and their use is problematical.

KIVA L

The height of kiva L is 7 feet 5 inches, that of the pilasters 5 feet 4 inches, and of the banquette 3 feet 3 inches. The diameter is 12 feet 2 inches. Number of pilasters 6. The flue opens on the western side; its height is 2 feet. Only a single mural niche was recognizable.

The walls of this kiva were very badly damaged, the whole of its front having fallen inward, covering the floor. The construction of the room demanded considerable rock cutting, especially on the eastern side, to secure the requisite depth. Whatever masonry remained in position was, as a rule, good. Probably no kiva in Cliff Palace was more dilapidated when work began. It had been used as a dump by those who had mutilated the ruins, and a great opening had been torn in its western wall. Excavations showed that the floor had been wholly destroyed.

KIVA N

The height of kiva N is 7 feet 4 inches, and that of the pilasters 5 feet 4 inches. The banquette is 3 feet high. The diameter of the kiva is 11 feet. There are 6 pilasters and 5 mural niches.

This kiva was in bad condition when the work began, but it is now in good repair and exhibits interesting features. The deflector was wholly destroyed, and it was impossible to find the sipapû. There are evidences of considerable rock cutting on the northern

---

[a] This kiva, one of the finest and in some features the most exceptional in Cliff Palace, is not indicated in Nordenskiöld's plan.

[b] Nordenskiöld describes a ventilator constructed in the same way.

side, and of a little on the eastern and southwestern sides. The kiva walls are blackened by smoke.

The height of kiva P is 8 feet, its diameter 11 feet 3 inches. The height from the floor to the top of a pilaster is 5 feet 10 inches, and to the top of the banquette 3 feet 4 inches. The number of pilasters is 6, and their average breadth about 20 inches.

From the flue to the deflector the distance is 2 feet 8 inches, and the deflector is situated 6 inches from the fire-hole. There are 5 mural niches.

The walls of this kiva are much blackened by smoke. The masonry is fair, but much broken on the northern and western sides. There is evidence that a considerable amount of rock has been pecked away on the northern side to the floor level. The kiva occupies almost the whole open space in which it is constructed, and the walls of neighboring buildings surround it on all sides, rising from the edge of the kiva. In order to secure a level foundation, parallel beams to support the floor were laid from a projecting rock to a masonry wall. The ends of these logs project above the path that leads to the main entrance.

This kiva (pl. 19) is round in shape and measures 8 feet 6 inches from the floor to the top of the wall. There were formerly eight pilasters, which averaged 18 inches in breadth. The height of the pilasters is 6 feet, and of the top of the banquette 3 feet 3 inches. The diameter of the kiva is 13 feet 8 inches.

The fire-hole is 22 inches from the deflector; the thickness of the latter is 10 inches, and its width 3 feet 3 inches. There are four mural niches, all in fine condition. Although the masonry of this kiva is the finest in Cliff Palace, its whole western end is destroyed. The floor west of the deflector has a slightly convex surface.[a]

No ceremonial opening, or sipapû, such as occurs in several other Cliff Palace kivas, was found in kiva Q. At the place where this feature usually appears the floor was broken, but as several of the Cliff Palace kivas have no specialized sipapûs it is possible that this device may be looked for in another opening in the floor. There are no sipapûs in the Hano kivas of the East Mesa of the Hopi, and the priests of that pueblo assert that the Tewa have no special hole in the kiva floor to represent this ceremonial opening. Apparently the Pueblos of the Rio Grande are like the Tewa of Hano in this respect. All the kivas of Spruce-tree House and a number of those

---

[a] In ceremonial rooms of ruins in the Navaho National Monument this curve is represented by a raised step.

in Cliff Palace have this ceremonial opening, thus following the Hopi rather than the Tewa custom. Whether the fireplace was used by those who performed rites in kiva Q as a symbolic opening into or from the " underworld " is unknown to the writer. The subterranean passage in kiva V leading to the fire-hole, but not entering it, is interesting in this particular. Kiva V, however, as pointed out, has in addition to the fire-hole a fine pottery-lined sipapû corresponding to the sipapûs in Hopi kivas, but made in the solid rock floor.

KIVA S

This kiva is square, with rounded corners. Its height is 8 feet, and the height of one of the pilasters above the floor 5 feet 10 inches. The banquettes are 3 feet 3 inches above the floor. The diameter of the kiva is 10 feet 4 inches.

The number of pilasters is 6; their average breadth is 20 inches. The distance from flue to deflector, which is a slab of stone, is 3 feet 2 inches; the height of the deflector is 1 foot 7 inches and its width 3 feet.

From the deflector to the fire-hole the distance is 7 inches. The diameter of the fire-hole is 2 feet, its depth 9 inches. There are 2 mural niches. The large banquette is 3 feet 6 inches broad. The shaft of the flue, after passing 18 inches under the kiva wall, turns southeastward 4 feet 4 inches and then takes a vertical course. The masonry of kiva S is fairly good. A jar is set into one of the banquettes, and was perhaps formerly used for containing sacred meal.[a] This receptacle was left as found, and a slab of stone placed slantingly above it to shield it from falling stones. Under the huge rock above it there are light masonry walls outlining diminutive rooms used possibly for storage but not for habitation.

KIVA T

This kiva stands on an elevated rock, and has double walls, the intervals between the wall of the kiva and the outside walls being filled with rubble.

The height of kiva T is 7 feet 6 inches, that of one of the pilasters 6 feet 6 inches. The banquette is 3 feet 9 inches above the floor. The diameter of the kiva is 10 feet 5 inches. There were probably 6

---

[a] Among the Hopi at the present day certain fetishes, as the effigies of the Great Plumed Serpent, are regarded as so sacred that when not in use they are kept in jars set in a banquette, the surface of which is level with the neck of the jar. These receptacles are closely sealed with a stone slab when the images are deposited in them. Possibly the jars set in the kiva banquettes of Cliff Palace may have been used for a similar purpose: i. e., were receptacles for fetishes held in such veneration that, as is the case with the Great Serpent effigies of the Hopi, one even touching them may, in the belief of the people, be afflicted with direful disorders.

pilasters and 2 mural niches. Although the greater part of the walls of this kiva was destroyed, a deep banquette still remains above the air shaft. The floor has the same level as the second terrace, or one story above kiva S, the roof of which is consequently at the level of the floor of kiva T.

Kiva T was in bad condition when work began, as part of its front wall had fallen and only the tops of the others were visible above the débris. Even the floor level was difficult to determine.

KIVA U

The form of kiva U is round, and its height is 7 feet 6 inches. The height of one of the pilasters is 4 feet 11 inches, and that of the banquette 3 feet 4 inches. The diameter of the kiva is 12 feet. There are 5 pilasters. The fire-hole is 4 inches from the flue; the diameter of the fire-hole is 20 inches, its depth 6 inches. There are 6 mural niches, so arranged that two large niches are situated above two small ones. The presence of but 5 pedestals is accounted for by the joining of 2 above the flue. Much rock-cutting was necessary in constructing this kiva, especially on the northern and southwestern sides. As the front wall of the kiva had fallen, it had to be practically rebuilt. The foundations were unstable, apparently having been constructed on loose stones carelessly laid.

KIVA V

This kiva is round and measures 5 feet 6 inches from the floor to the top of one of the pilasters. The top of the banquette is 3 feet 4 inches above the floor. The diameter of the kiva is 12 feet 8 inches. The number of pilasters is 6 and their average breadth 20 inches.

The distance from the deflector to the line of the wall is 23 inches; the height of the deflector is 22 inches, the thickness 9 inches, and the width 3 feet 2 inches. The fire-hole is 18 inches from the sipapû; the latter is 10 inches deep and 3 inches in diameter, and is lined with a pottery tube cemented in place. There are three mural niches.

Kiva V is exceptional in the amount of rock-cutting that was necessary for lowering the floor to the desired level. Probably the greatest amount of stone-cutting was done in this kiva.

There remains to be mentioned a unique tunnel which may eventually throw some light on ceremonial openings in the kivas of cliff-dwellings. Just beneath the adobe floor, extending from a vertical flue outside the kiva to the fire-hole, which it does not, however, enter, there is a passage through which a small person may crawl. Exteriorly this opens into a vertical flue which was broken down; inside it ends bluntly at the fire-hole. About midway of its length there extends from it a lateral passageway, slightly curved, forming a well-worn doorway. This curved passage opens through the kiva floor by a manhole. The walls of these passages are constructed of good masonry. Their function is unknown, but as most structures connected with kivas are ceremonial, this may provisionally be called a ceremonial opening.

It is evident that this ceremonial passage had nothing to do or at least had no connection with the ventilator and deflector of the kiva. The opening is situated under the floor, passing in its course beneath the deflector, and its external opening is by a vertical passage outside the ventilator. It also differs from the ventilator in having a lateral branch likewise situated under the floor. Passing to kivas outside the Mesa Verde region, we find homologous passages recorded as present under the floor in Pueblo Bonito, a ruin on the Chaco, and in the kiva of a ruin not far from Chama, where the passage under the floor is excavated in solid rock. Evidently we have in this structure a ceremonial opening the true significance of which is yet to be determined. Is it connected with the Tewa concept that the fire-hole is a sipapû, or was it used in fire rites that were performed about the fireplace? These and other questions that might be proposed must remain unanswered until more is known of similar passages in other cliff-dwelling kivas.

A SUBTYPE OF KIVA (KIVA M)

The method of roof construction, which is the main difference that distinguishes a kiva of the subtype from one of the first type, is due to the absence of pilasters. Kiva M of Cliff Palace may be assigned to this subtype, although many examples of it occur in ruins farther down the San Juan, as well as in the Navaho National Monument and in Canyon de Chelly. Kivas of the subtype are similar to those of the second type in that pilasters are absent, but they differ from them in the presence of a large banquette and in the subterranean position, which features also characterize the first type. The only circular kivas known to the ruins near the East Mesa of the Hopi of Arizona belong to the first type, two of which are found at Kukuchomo, the two ruins on the summit of the mesa above Sikyatki.

The method of roofing a kiva of the subtype may be clearly observed in the kiva of Scaffold House in the Navaho National Monument.[a] The rafters here are parallel, and extend across the top of the kiva, their ends resting on the woll. The middle beam, which is the largest, is flanked on each side by another. Upon these supporting beams are laid others at right angles, and on these were placed the brush, bark, and clay that covered the roof. Entrance

---

[a] See *Bulletin 50, Bureau of American Ethnology.*

was gained by means of a hatchway on one side of the roof near the large banquette, which occupies a position, as respects the entrance and the place supposedly occupied by the ladder and the fire-pit, similar to the spectator's platform of a modern rectangular Hopi kiva, except that it is higher above the floor and is relatively smaller. If the banquettes were depressed and enlarged into a platform, the form of the kiva being changed from circular to rectangular, thus modified the banquette would form a structure like the spectator's platform of a typical modern Hopi kiva.[a]

Perhaps of all the ceremonial rooms repaired the walls of kiva M were in the most dangerous condition. The front of the northern wall of room 39 had been undermined and was without foundation, hanging without basal support except at the ends. A support was constructed under this hanging wall, and to give additional strength the foundations were rebuilt a little broader at the base than formerly, causing the wall to bulge almost imperceptibly into the kiva. Although no pilasters were seen, the deep banquette on the northwestern side places it among the kivas of the first type.

KIVAS OF THE SECOND TYPE

The architecture of the two kivas O and R are so different from those already considered that they are set apart from the others in a second type. The form and structure of kiva W indicate that this room also may be classed as of the same type. In the side canyon north of that in which Cliff Palace is situated, where water was obtained throughout the summer, there is another kiva, also supposed to belong to the second type.[b]

The main difference in construction between the two types of kivas is the absence of pilasters, which implies the absence of a roof in the second type. The suggestion that a kiva of the second type is simply an unfinished form of the first type has little to support it, but whether the architectural difference in the two types has any functional importance or meaning is unknown. It has been suggested that one type was used by the Winter, the other by the Summer people.[c]

---

[a] The two circular kivas of Kukuchomo, near Sikyatki, have this large banquette and in other respects resemble the ruins of Canyon de Chelly. Kukuchomo marks the site of a settlement of the Coyote clan of the Hopi in prehistoric times.

[b] As a huge rock had fallen from the roof of the cave in which this kiva lies, since it was first occupied, it would appear that the place was abandoned on that account.

[c] Nordenskiöld's description of this kiva has been quoted earlier in this paper. In the description of a ceremonial room of a somewhat similar or of the same type in Spruce-tree House the term " warrior room " is used; there is nothing to warrant this designation, however, and it would be better to consider it simply as a kiva of the second type.

KIVA O

Kiva O is rounded below and square above, with a north-south diameter of 11 feet 10 inches, and an east-west diameter of 10 feet 6 inches. The ventilator opens in the western wall. There are 2 mural niches.

Both the plastered floor and the deflector are lacking, and there is no fire-hole nor sipapû. No roof or pilasters to support it were detected. It is difficult to measure the surrounding wall on account of its varying height. The masonry is good, but there are no signs on the walls that a fire had ever burned within the chamber. It would appear that this kiva was roofless, and that it had broad banquettes at the northern and southern sides.

KIVA R

In shape this kiva is oval below and square above, without pilasters or other evidences of a roof. There are no signs of a floor, a deflector, or a fire-hole. The surrounding wall of the kiva is high; apparently there was an entrance at the eastern side. Banquettes are present on the northern and southern ends, and a narrow ledge skirts the other two sides.

There are 4 mural niches: (1) south by east, measuring 15 by 11 by 13 inches; (1) north by east, measuring 11½ by 8 by 15 inches; (2) in the north wall, measuring 13 by 8 by 12 inches, and 12 by 8 by 13 inches; the latter three being placed in a row and separated by slabs of stone. In the south wall there is a tunnel terminating bluntly and bifurcated at the end.

Although kiva R was regarded by Nordenskiöld as furnishing evidence of a transition form connecting circular and rectangular kivas, it seems to the author a new type rather than a modification of the circular or the rectangular kivas.

KIVA W

Kiva W is not generally included among the Cliff Palace ceremonial rooms on account of its isolation from the houses, but there is no doubt that it should be so enumerated. It lies about 50 feet west of the end of the last room in the cliff-dwelling, and is not accompanied with secular rooms. Although situated on the same level as the houses, its walls rise two tiers high, but no part of the inclosure is subterranean.

From the height of the walls it at first seemed as if in kiva W there were evidences of a room above. This condition would be contrary to the rule and, to the Hopi mind, ceremonially impossible; but if its upper walls are regarded as homogeneous with the high walls that surround kivas O and R, and we interpret this as an example of the second type of kiva, the anomaly is explained.

Although this kiva is placed provisionally in the second type mainly because of these lofty side walls, on account of its isolation at the end of Cliff Palace several observers have not regarded it as belonging to the ruin. Neither Nordenskiöld nor Morley and Kidder included it in their ground plans, nor does Nordenskiöld mention it in his enumeration of Cliff Palace kivas.

As kiva W is almost wholly unprotected by the cave roof, its walls have greatly suffered from the downpour of rains to which they are exposed. The masonry is fairly good. Evidently it was an important building, and was isolated from other rooms possibly for some special purpose. As there are few or no walls of secular rooms near it, one may believe that it was resorted to by the villagers on special occasions and did not belong to any one clan.

MINOR ANTIQUITIES

In the preceding pages have been described the major antiquities, such as walls and those permanent objects which could not be removed from the places where they were constructed without more or less harm. There remain to be considered the minor antiquities, or the smaller objects which are movable and of a more perishable nature, especially if left in the places where they were found. It was mainly in search of such objects that much of the mutilation of Cliff Palace was done.

It was not expected that excavations would yield any considerable number of specimens, since for years Cliff Palace had been dug over in search of them, and many hundreds of objects had already been found and carried away to be sold either to museums or to individuals. Notwithstanding these unfavorable conditions, the collection of objects, now deposited in the National Museum, is sufficient to afford some idea of the culture of the Cliff Palace people.

Among the objects that may be mentioned in the category of minor antiquities are pottery, basketry, implements of stone, bone, and wood, fabrics of various kinds, ornaments, fetishes, and the like—all those objects commonly called artifacts that make up collections from cliff-dwellings generally.

The excavations at Cliff Palace have revealed no specimens strikingly different from those already described as from Spruce-tree House. We would expect some variation in the symbols on pottery from the two ruins, but the differences are not conspicuous in the few specimens that have been compared. Nor is there any peculiarity in the form of the pottery, as the ceramic objects from Cliff Palace practically duplicate those from Spruce-tree House, already described, and probably are not much unlike those still buried in Long House, Balcony House, and the House with the Square Tower.

As many ceremonial objects, being highly prized, may have been removed from Cliff Palace when the place was deserted by its inhabitants, the few that remained present scant material from which to add to our knowledge of the ceremonial life of the people. The existence of so many kivas would point to many rites, although a large number of sacred rooms does not necessarily indicate more complex or elaborate rites than a smaller number: multiplicity of kivas does not necessarily mean multiplicity of ceremonies, nor few kivas a limited ritual. In no pueblo are there more complicated ceremonies than at Walpi, where there are only five of these sacred rooms; but it must be remembered that many of the religious rites of Walpi are performed in kihus, or secular rooms. The same may have been true of Cliff Palace.

The writer's belief is that in historic times, by which is meant since the advent of missionaries, altars have become more elaborate and rites more complex at Walpi than in prehistoric times, and that through the same influence the use of images or idols has also increased. This increase in the complexity of rites may be traced to the amalgamation of clans or to a substitution of the fraternities of priesthoods for simple clan ancestor worship. The elaborate character of ceremonial paraphernalia may likewise be due to acculturation,[a] which increases in complication with the lapse of time.

STONE IMPLEMENTS

The stone implements from Cliff Palace consist of axes, mauls, paint grinders, pecking stones, metates, balls, flakes, spear and arrow points, and various other articles (pls. 20–22). There is great uniformity in these implements, the axes, for instance, being generally single edged, although a good specimen of double-edged hatchet is in the collection. A fragment of the peculiar stone implement called *tcamahia*[b] by the Hopi was found.

While as a rule the hatchets are without handles, one specimen (pl. 20) is exceptional in this particular. The handle of this hatchet from Cliff Palace, like that from Spruce-tree House, elsewhere described, is a stick bent in a loop around the stone head.

---

[a] For instance, the complicated reredos of many of the modern Hopi altars is made of flat wooden slabs, the manufacture of which would be very difficult for a people ignorant of iron. These probably replaced painted stone slabs of simpler character, examples of which have been found in ruins and indeed still survive in some of the oldest rites.

[b] This object probably came from near Tokónabi, the ancient home of the Snake people of Walpi, on San Juan river. Fourteen of these *tcamahias* form part of the Antelope altar in the Snake Dance at Walpi.

POUNDING STONES

Anyone who will examine the amount of stone-cutting necessary to lower the floor of kiva V, for instance, to its present depth, or to peck away the projecting rock in some of the other kivas, will realize at once that the Cliff Palace people were industrious stone workers. A number of the pounding stones (pl. 22, *a*) with which this work was done have been found. These stones are cubical in form, or rounded or pointed at one end or both ends, and provided with two or more pits on the sides. They were evidently held directly in the hand and used without handles. Although generally small, they sometimes are of considerable size. The stone of which they are made is foreign to the vicinity; it is hard, as would be absolutely necessary to be effectual in the use to which they were put.

GRINDING STONES

The most common variety of grinding stones is, of course, the metate, or mill-stone, used in grinding corn. These implements have a variety of forms. They may be flat above and rounded below, or flat on both sides, triangular on each face, or simply convex on each side. None of them have feet like the Mexican metates. The stone with which the grinding was done, or the one held in the hand, also varies in shape, size, and evidences of use.[a] Stones with a depression in one face served as mortars. A stone in the form of a pestle, flat on the end, served as a paint grinder. Several flat stones with smooth surface, showing the effect of grinding, and others with slight concavities, undoubtedly served the same purpose. Smooth stones showing grinding on one or more faces were evidently the implements with which the builders smoothed the walls of the houses after the masonry had been laid; others were used in polishing pottery.

MISCELLANEOUS STONES

Many stone balls, large or small, were found. Some of these show chipping, others are ground smooth. Certain of these balls were evidently used in a game popular at Cliff Palace, in which they were rolled or dropped into deep pits and grooves. It appears that this game was played by occupants of the sacred rooms, as the pits are common in the kiva floors. Other stone balls were formerly tied to the end of a handle with a thong of hide and used as a weapon.

---

[a] At several places on the surfaces of projecting rocks forming the foundations of buildings may be noticed grooves where metates were sharpened. One or more of these occur at the entrance to the " street " in front of room 51. The foundation of a wall in one room was built directly upon one of these grooves, part of the groove being in sight, the rest covered with masonry. Near room 92 there are many of these grooves as well as small pits.

A half oval stone, smooth and flat at one pole, is supposed to have been an idol, possibly the earth goddess, who is repeatedly represented by the Hopi in a similar way. It was left near where it was found at the northwest corner of kiva H. Our masons used rectangular slabs of soft stone, which were doubtless door-closes, as mortar boards. They were held in place in the door opening by jambs made of mortar laid on sticks, and by a horizontal rod which passed between two osier eyelets set in the uprights of the door-frame and projecting from it. These stone doors were sometimes held in place by a groove cut in the threshold or by a ledge of adobe.

Two thin, flat, circular stone disks (pl. 22, c), with smooth surfaces and square edges, accompanied the calcined human bones in the inclosure at the northern end of the large refuse heap. It is probable that some of these disks were used as covers for mortuary vases. Irregularly shaped flat stones with pits and incised figures pecked in their surface were used in a game, and a slab covered with incised figures but without the pits (pl. 23, c) probably served a similar purpose.

Several large stones, which the builders of Cliff Palace had begun to dress and had later rejected, show the method adopted by them in cutting stones the required size. When stones were found to be too large to be laid, or had projections that interfered with the required shape, a groove was pecked where the fracture was desired and the stone broken along the groove.

POTTERY

No ruin in the Mesa Verde National Park has yielded more specimens of pottery than Cliff Palace, many pieces of which are preserved in various museums in Colorado and elsewhere. The collection gathered by the writer was small compared with some of these, and although only a few whole pieces were found, by restoration from fragments a fair number of specimens, ample perhaps for generalization, were procured. In the following mention of the pottery obtained from the ruin a very comprehensive idea of the perfection in the ceramic art attained in Cliff Palace can hardly be hoped.

Southwestern pottery may be divided into two types, so far as superficial appearance goes: (1) coiled or indented undecorated ware; (2) smooth polished ware. Of the latter there are two subtypes: (a) pottery with a surface slip, generally white, on which designs are painted, and (b) decorated pottery without a superficial slip, and generally reddish in color. Cliff Palace pottery, when decorated, belongs to the last two divisions, but some of the best made specimens belong to the coiled or indented type. Although there are several fragments of red pottery ornamented with designs painted in black, and one or two specimens in which the basal color is orange, the majority of the specimens belong to the so-called black-and-white ware, which may therefore be called a type of this region.

The whole pieces of pottery collected were chiefly mortuary vessels, and probably contained food offerings, indicating, like the sipapûs in the kivas, that the cliff-dwellers had a distinct conception of a future life. In addition to the limited number of pieces of unbroken pottery, many of the fragments were decorated with novel patterns. Fragments of corrugated and indented ware are by far the most numerous, but although many of these were obtained, not a whole piece was found, with the exception of a single specimen plastered in a fire-hole and three others similarly fixed in the banquettes of kivas. These were left as they were found.

The same forms of pottery, as dippers, ladles, vases, canteens, jars, and similar objects, occur at Cliff Palace as at Spruce-tree House (pl. 23–27). All varieties were repeatedly found, some with old cracks that had been mended, and one is still tied with the yucca cord with which it had been repaired. It is evident from the frequency with which the Cliff Palace people mended their old pottery that they prized the old vessels and were very careful to preserve them, being loth to abandon even a cracked jar (pl. 23, d). None of the Cliff Palace pottery is glazed.[a] Some specimens of smooth pottery are coarse in texture and without decoration; others have elaborate geometrical figures; but animate objects are confined almost entirely to a few pictures of birds or other animals and rudely drawn human figures. The pictography of the pottery affords scant data bearing on the interpretation of the ancient symbolism of the inhabitants, as compared with that of Sikyatki, for example, in the Hopi country.

Food bowls.—In form the food bowls[b] from Cliff Palace (pls. 23–25) are the same as those from other prehistoric sites of the Southwest, but as a rule the Cliff Palace bowls are smaller than those of Sikyatki and the ruins on the Little Colorado. They have, as a rule, a thicker lip, which is square across instead of tapering to a thin edge or flaring, as is sometimes the case elsewhere. The surface, inside and out, is commonly very smooth, even glossy. The pottery was built up by coiling the clay, and the colors were made permanent by the firing.

---

[a] The first description of " glazed " pottery in the Pueblo region is given by Castañeda (1540), who says : " Throughout this province [Tiguex] are found glazed pottery and vessels truly remarkable both in shape and execution." This has sometimes been interpreted to mean the glossy but unglazed pottery of Santa Clara. Glazed pottery was found by the writer in 1896 in ruins on the Little Colorado. It appears to be intrusive in the Arizona ruins.

[b] Food bowls with handles, so common to the ruins of northern Arizona, were not found at Cliff Palace.

The basis of the study of symbolism was of course the pottery decoration. As a rule the center of the inside of the food bowls is plain, but several have this portion ornamented with squares, triangles, and other figures. The outside of several bowls from Cliff Palace and Spruce-tree House is decorated, notwithstanding Nordenskiöld speaks of exterior decoration as rare in his collections from the Mesa Verde. The geometric ornaments consist of rectangular figures.[a]

Mugs.—Some authors have questioned whether the prehistoric people of the Southwest were familiar with this form of pottery. The collections from Cliff Palace (pl. 24–26) and Spruce-tree House set at rest any reasonable doubt on this point. There are, however, peculiarities in the form of mugs from Mesa Verde. The diameter of the base is generally larger, tapering gently toward the mouth, and one end of the handle is rarely affixed to the rim. The inside of the mug is not usually decorated, but the exterior bears geometrical designs in which terraces, triangles, and parallel lines predominate. Curved lines are rare, and spirals are absent. Mugs with two handles are unrepresented. There are no ladles in the collection, but several broken handles of ladles were found in the refuse. One of these is decorated with a series of parallel, longitudinal, and transverse lines, a design as widely spread as Pueblo pottery, extending across the boundary into Mexico.

Globular Vessels.—The globular form of pottery was used for carrying water and seems to have been common at Cliff Palace. One of these vessels (pl. 25, *b*) has a small neck, and attached to it are two eyelets for insertion of the thong by which it was carried. Some of the globular vessels (pl. 25, *a*) have the neck small, the orifice wide, and the lip perforated with holes for strings. Double-lipped globular vessels, having a groove like that of a teapot, have been found in Cliff Palace as well as in other ruins of Mesa Verde and Montezuma canyon. The rims of these are generally perforated, as if for the insertion of thongs to facilitate carrying. The bottoms of these vessels are rarely concave. They are sometimes decorated on the outside, but never on the interior.

Vases.—Small vases with contracted neck and lip slightly curved, and larger vases with the same characters, occur sparingly. These (pls. 26, 27, *b*) are decorated on the exterior in geometrical designs; the interior is plain. The bases are rounded, sometimes flat, and in rare instances concave.

Disks.—Among pottery objects should be mentioned certain disks, some large, others small, some perforated in the middle, others imperforate. Several are decorated. These disks served as covers for bowls, and similar disks were employed as counters in games or as

---

[a] No curved lines are present in the many examples of decoration on the outside of food bowls from Sikyatki.

spindle whorls. None of the clay disks from Cliff Palace has a central knob or handle like those from Spruce-tree House.

RELATIONS AS DETERMINED BY POTTERY

In the report on Spruce-tree House, using pottery as a basis, the prehistoric culture of the Southwest, including the Gila-Salt area, which can not strictly be designated Pueblo, has been provisionally divided into several subcultural areas. Among these are the Hopi, a specialized modification of the Little Colorado, the Little Colorado proper, the San Juan, and the Gila-Salt areas.

Cliff Palace pottery symbols are not closely related to those on old Hopi ware, as typified by the collections from Sikyatki.[a] Neither Cliff Palace nor Spruce-tree House pottery is closely allied to that of the Little Colorado, as exemplified by Homolobi ware, but both have a closer likeness to that from Wukóki, a settlement ascribed to the Snake clans, situated near Black Falls, not far from Flagstaff, Arizona. As a rule the symbolism on pottery from the Little Colorado, which includes that of its upper tributaries, as the Zuñi, Puerco, Leroux, and Cottonwood washes, is a mixture of all types. This river valley has exerted a distributing influence in Pueblo migrations, and in its ruins are found symbols characteristic of many clans, some of which, following up the tributaries of the Salt and the Gila, have brought Casas Grandes decorative elements; others, with sources in the northeast, have contributed designs from an opposite direction. The predominating directions of ceramic culture migration in this valley have been from south to north and from west to east.[b]

The relation of Cliff Palace pottery designs to the symbolism or decorative motives characteristic of the Gila valley ruins is remote. Several geometrical patterns are common to all areas of the Southwest, but specialized features characterize each of these areas. The pottery from Cliff Palace finds its nearest relation throughout the upper San Juan region; the most distant to that of ruins in northern Arizona near Colorado Grande.[c]

---

[a] Sikyatki ware is more closely related to that of the ancient Jemez and Pajarito subarea than to that made by the Snake clans when they lived at Tokónabi, their old home, or at Black Falls shortly before they arrived at Walpi. Careful study of ancient Walpi pottery made by the Bear clan before the arrival of the Snake clans shows great similarity to Sikyatki pottery, and the same holds regarding the ware from old Shongopovi.

[b] In the ruins found on the banks of the Little Colorado at Black Falls, the predominating influence, as shown by pottery symbols, has been from the north. It is known from legends that Wukóki was settled by clans from the north, the close likeness to the symbols of the San Juan valley supporting traditions still current at Walpi.

[c] A thorough comparative study of Pueblo pottery symbolism is much restricted on account of lack of material from all ceramic culture areas of the Southwest. It is likewise made difficult by a mixture of types produced by the migration of clans from one area to another. The subject is capable of scientific treatment, but at present is most difficult of analysis.

SYMBOLS ON POTTERY

The symbols on the Cliff Palace pottery are reducible to rectangular geometrical figures; life forms, with the rare exceptions noted above, are not represented, and the exceptional examples are crude. Contrast this condition with the pottery from Sikyatki, where three-fourths of the decorations are life designs, as figures of men or animals, many of which are highly symbolic. The "sky band" with hanging bird design, peculiar to old Hopi ware, was unknown to Cliff Palace potters. Encircling lines are unbroken, no specimen being found with the break so common to the pottery from the Hopi, Little Colorado, Gila, and Jemez subareas. The designs on food bowls are often accompanied with marginal dots. No example of the conventionalized "breath-feather" so common in Sikyatki pottery decoration occurs. Spattering with color was not practiced.

An analysis of the pottery decorations shows that the dominant forms may be reduced to a few types, of which the terrace, the spiral, the triangle, and the cross in its various forms are the most common.

Various forms and sizes of triangles, singly or in combination, constitute one of the most constant devices used by the cliff-dwellers of the Mesa Verde in the decoration of their pottery. It is common to find two series of triangles arranged on parallel lines. When the component triangles are right-angled they sometimes alternate with each other, forming a zigzag which may be sinistral or dextral. This design may be called an alternate right-angular figure.

If instead of two parallel series of right-angle triangles there are isosceles triangles, they may be known as alternate isosceles triangles. These triangles, when opposite, form a series of hour-glass figures or squares. This form is commonly accompanied by a row of dots, affixed to top and base, known as the dotted square or hour-glass figure. Hour-glass designs are commonly represented upright, but the angles of the triangles may be so placed that the series is horizontal, forming a continuous chain. Often the bases of these serially arrayed hour-glass figures are separated by rows of dots or by blank spaces.

A row of triangles, each so placed that the angles touch the middles of the sides of others in the same series, form an arc called linear triangles. The St. Andrews cross, which occurs sparingly on Mesa Verde pottery, is formed by joining the vertical angles of four isosceles triangles.

The cross and the various forms of the familiar swastika also occur on Cliff Palace pottery. The star symbol, made up of four squares so arranged as to leave a space in the middle, is yet to be found in Mesa Verde. Parallel curved lines, crooked at the end or combined with triangles and squares, occur commonly in the pottery decoration

of Cliff Palace. S-shaped figures are known. Rectangles or tri
angles with dots, or even a line of dots alone, are not rare in the decu-
ration. No designs representing leaves or flowers occur on pottery
from Cliff Palace, nor has the spider-web pattern been found. The
most common geometrical decorations are the stepped or terraced
figures, generally called rain-clouds.

POTTERY RESTS

Among the objects found in the refuse heaps of Cliff Palace are
rings, about 6 inches in diameter, woven of corn husks or cedar bark
bound together with fiber of yucca or other plants. These rings (pl.
28) were evidently used as supports for earthenware vases, the bases
of which are generally rounded, so that otherwise they would not
stand upright. Similar rings may have been used by the women in
carrying jars of water on their heads,[a] as among the Zuñi of to-day.
Some of these rings may have been used in what is called the
" ring and dart " game, which is often ceremonial in nature. The best
made of all these objects, found by Mr. Fuller on his visit to a
neighboring canyon, is shown in the accompanying illustration
(pl. 28, b). The specimen is made of tightly woven corn husks,
around which the fiber is gathered so as to form an equatorial ridge
rarely present in these objects.

BASKETRY

A few instructive specimens of basketry or wicker ware were
exhumed at Cliff Palace. One of the most interesting of these is
the unfinished plaque shown in the accompanying figure 2.
One specimen of basketry (pl. 29) has the form of a hopper; its
whole central part was purposely omitted, but the basket is finished
on the inner and outer margins. It recalls a basket used by the Ute
and other Shoshonean Indians, but it is different in form from any
figured in Nordenskiöld's work, and, so far as the author is acquainted
with other specimens of basketry from Mesa Verde ruins, is unique.
It is supposed that when used this hopper was placed on a flat or
rounded stone and that corn or other seeds to be pounded were placed
in it, the stone thus forming the surface upon which the seeds were
treated, and the sides of the basket serving to retain the meal.

SANDALS

The sandals found at Cliff Palace (pls. 30–32) are practically the
same in form, material, and weave as those recorded from Spruce-
tree House. The shape of these, however, is particularly instruc-

---

[a] The Hopi use large clay canteens for this purpose, no vessels resembling which,
whole or in fragments, have been found at Cliff Palace.

tive, as it appears to shed light on the meaning of certain flat stones, rare in cliff-dwellings, called "sandal lasts." These stones, one of which is figured in the report on Spruce-tree House, are rectangular, flat, thin, smooth, with rounded corners, and sometimes have a notch in the rim at one end. The exceptionally formed sandal from Cliff Palace (pl. 32) is similar in shape and has a notch identical with that of the problematical stone objects, supporting the theory that the latter were used as sandal lasts, as interpreted by several authors.

The sandals are ordinarily made of plaited yucca leaves, their upper side being sometimes covered with corn leaves for protection of

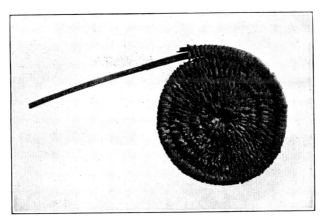

Fig. 2.—Coil of basket plaque.

the feet. The thongs that passed between the toes are made either of yucca or other vegetable fiber, or of hide.

WOODEN OBJECTS

There are several objects made of wood in the collection from Cliff Palace, some of the least problematical of which are long, pointed rods (fig. 3) with which the ancients probably made the holes in which they planted corn, in much the same way as the Hopi plant at the present day. These implements are commonly pointed at the end, but one or two are broadened and flattened. No example of the spatular variety of dibble found by others, and none showing the point of attachment of a flat stone blade, occurs in the collection. One or two short broken sticks, having a knob cut on the unbroken end, are interpreted as handles of weapons—a use that is not definitely proven. There are several sticks that evidently were used for barring windows or for holding stone door-closes in place.

Among problematical wooden objects may be mentioned billets (pl. 33), flattened on one side and rounded at each end. Two of these were found, with calcined human bones, in the inclosure used for cremation of the dead, situated at the northern end of the large refuse heap. These, like the bowls with which they were associated, were coated with a white salt-like deposit. None of the many wooden objects figured by Nordenskiöld are exactly the same as those above mentioned, although the one shown in his plate XLIII, figure 17, is very close in form and size.

Several bent twigs or loops of flexible wood from the refuse heaps were found; these are supposed to have been inserted in the masonry, one on each side of door and window openings, to hold in place the stick which served as a bolt for fastening the door or window stone in position.

Bent sticks, of dumb-bell shape, having a knob at each end (pl. 33, *b*), are believed to have been used in games. A similar object from the Mancos region is figured by Mr. Stewart Culin in his account of the games of the cliff-dwellers.[a] The ancient people of the semi-deserts of Atacama, in South America, employed a similar but larger

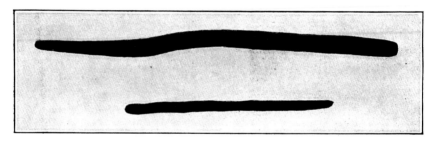

Fig. 3.—Planting sticks.

stick, to which cords were attached for strapping bundles on their beasts of burden.

DRILLS

A small pointed stone attached with fiber to the end of a stick, similar to those found by Nordenskiöld in ruin 9 and at Long House, was found.

The Cliff Palace people kindled fire by means of the fire-drill and fire-stick (hearth), a specimen of which, similar to one collected at Spruce-tree House, is contained in the collection. Both of these fire-making implements were broken when found, apparently thrown away on that account either by the original people or by subsequent visitors.

BONE IMPLEMENTS

Many bone implements (pl. 34, 35) were found during the excavation of Cliff Palace. They are of the bones of birds and small mammals, or, now and then, of those of antelope or bear, the latter fur-

---

[a] *Twenty-fourth Annual Report of the Bureau of American Ethnology.*

nishing the best material for large scrapers. These implements were evidently sharpened by rubbing on the stones of walls or on the face of the cliff, as grooves, apparently made in this way, are there visible in several places. Scratches made in shaping or sharpening bones, repeatedly found on the masonry of Cliff Palace, are not peculiar, resembling those referred to in the report on Spruce-tree House. A small tube with a hole midway of its length doubtless served as a whistle, similar instruments being still often used in Hopi ceremonies to imitate the calls of birds.

Sections of bones were found tied in pairs, and while it is not clear that these were threaded on a cord and worn as necklaces or armlets, as Nordenskiöld suggests, they may have been tied side by side, forming a kind of breastplate not unlike that used by the Plains tribes. In a room of Spruce-tree House, according to Nordenskiöld, eight similar pieces of bone were found strung on a fine thong of hide.

Among other bone objects there is one, of unknown use, about an inch long and one-fourth of an inch in diameter, nearly cylindrical in shape. A bone with a hole in one end, similar to those figured by Nordenskiöld, forms part of the collection.

TURQUOISE EAR PENDANTS AND OTHER OBJECTS

The single specimen of turquoise found at Cliff Palace was probably an ear pendant, and a black jet bead was apparently used for the same purpose. With the polished cylinder of hematite found one can still paint the face or body a reddish color, as the Hopi do with a similar object. From the sipapû of kiva D there was taken a small deerskin bag, tied with yucca fiber and containing a material resembling iron pyrites, evidently an offering of some kind to the gods of the underworld.

A button made of lignite, and beads of the same material, were found in the refuse heap in front of the ruin after a heavy rain. The former is broken, but it resembles that found at Spruce-tree House, although it is not so finely made, and also one from Homólobi, a ruin on the Little Colorado, near Winslow, Arizona.

SEEDS

The cobs and seeds of corn, squash and pumpkin seeds, beans, and fragments of gourds give some idea of the vegetable products known to the Cliff Palace people. Corn furnished the most important food of the people, and its dried leaves, stalks, and tassels were abundant in all parts of their refuse heaps. Naturally, in a cave where many small rodents have lived for years, it is rare to find seed corn above ground that has not been appropriated by these animals, and in the dry, alkaline bone-phosphate dust edible corn is not very common, although now and then occurs a cob with attached seeds. The corn of Cliff Palace, already figured by Nordenskiöld, resembles that still cultivated by some of the Hopi.

FIG. 4.—Woven forehead band.

TEXTILES

The Cliff Palace people manufactured fairly good cloth, the component cords or strings being of two or three strands and well twisted. So finely made and durable are some of these cords that they might be mistaken for white men's work; some of them, however, are very coarse, and are tied in hanks. Among varieties of cords may be mentioned those wound with feathers, from which textiles, ordinarily called "feather cloth," was made. Yucca and cotton were employed in the manufacture of almost all kinds of fabrics. A few fragments of netting were found.

The finest cloth was manufactured from cotton, a good specimen of which, showing a pattern woven in different colors, is contained in the collection.

Several woven belts, and also a head-band similar to that figured in the report on Spruce-tree House, were uncovered by the excavations. The largest fragment of cloth was taken out of the crematory, or inclosure containing the calcined human bones, at the northern end of the larger refuse heap. It appears to have been a portion of a bag, or possibly of a head covering, but it is so fragmentary that its true use is unknown. The pattern is woven in darker colored threads, with a selvage at two ends. The material out of which it was made has not been definitely determined, but it closely resembles that of the specimen figured by Nordenskiöld (plate L) from Mug House. Our excavations were rewarded with a fine woven head-band with loops at the ends (fig. 4), similar to that described and figured in the report on Spruce-tree House. Several small fragments of cloth were recovered from the refuse heap, but none of them was large enough to indicate the form of the garment to which they originally belonged.

In the group of fabrics may be included nets and cloth with feathers wound around warp and woof, similar to those figured from Spruce-tree House.

There were several specimens of yucca strings, tied in loops, generally six in number, which presumably were devoted to the same purpose as by the present Hopi, who attach to the string six ears of corn, representing the cardinal points on the six-directions altar, and hang them on the walls of a priest's house. If the cliff-dwellers used this string for a similar purpose, it would appear that they, like the Hopi, recognized six cardinal points—north, west, south, east, above, and below—and worshiped gods of these directions, to which they erected altars.[a]

HUMAN BURIALS

As has been seen, there were two methods of disposing of the dead—by inhumation and by cremation. The former may have been either house burial or burial in the refuse heaps in the rear of the buildings. With both forms of disposing of the dead mortuary food offerings were found. Evidences of prehistoric burials and cremation were found both on the mesa above Cliff Palace and in the ruin.[b]

The practice of cremation among the cliff-dwellers has long been known. Nordenskiöld writes (p. 49):

That cremation, however, was sometimes practiced by the Cliff Dwellers seems probable from the fact that Richard Wetherill observed in the same ruin, when the above-mentioned burial chamber was found, bodies which had apparently been burnt, together with the pottery belonging to the dead.

The evidences of cremation found in the inclosure at the northern end of the refuse space of Cliff Palace is conclusive. The calcined bones uncovered here were also accompanied with mortuary pottery, cloth, and wooden objects.

The flexed position of the bodies of the dead occurs constantly in the earth burials, which may be explained by the almost universal

---

[a] For a Hopi six-directions altar, see *Journal of American Ethnology and Archæology,* Vol. II, 1892.

[b] The house burials appear to have been mainly those of priests or other important personages.

belief among primitive people that when the body is returned to
" mother earth " it should be placed in the posture it normally had
before birth. In house burials at Spruce-tree House the bodies were
sometimes extended at full length, which may be interpreted to mean
that the dead were not returned to the earth mother. There was no
uniformity of posture in the burials at Cliff Palace.

The work at Cliff Palace was undertaken at too late a day to
recover any mummified human remains, all having been previously
removed. Nordenskiöld's figures and descriptions of desiccated
human bodies from other Mesa Verde cliff-dwellings would apply,
in a measure, to those from Cliff Palace.

CONCLUSIONS

While the work of excavation and repair of Cliff Palace described
in the preceding pages adds nothing distinctly new to existing knowledge of cliff-dweller culture, it renders a more comprehensive idea
of the conditions of life in one of the largest of these interesting
ancient settlements in our Southwest. Of all the questions that present themselves after a work of this kind, perhaps the most important, from a scientific point of view, is, What relation exists between
the culture of Cliff Palace and that of the neighboring pueblos?
Directly across the canyon, in full view of Cliff Palace, there is a
typical pueblo ruin, almost identical in character with many others
scattered throughout the Southwest, some of which are known to
have been inhabited in historic times by ancestors of Pueblo peoples
still living. The contribution here made to the knowledge of cliff-
dwelling culture will, it is hoped, shed light on the question, In
what way are the cliff-dwellers and the Pueblos related?

The relationship in culture of the former people of Cliff Palace
to those of the large pueblo ruin on the mesa across the canyon is
most instructive. How were the inhabitants of these two settlements
related; and were the two sites inhabited simultaneously, or is the
pueblo ruin older than Cliff Palace? So far as the culture of the
inhabitants of the two is known (and knowledge of the pueblo is
scant), the two settlements were synchronously inhabited, but nothing in them gives indication of the period of their occupancy. These
questions can be settled only by the excavation of this pueblo or of
some similar ruin on the plateau.[a] Nordenskiöld, with the data

---

[a] A true comparison of the mesa habitation and the cliff-dwelling can be made only by
renewed work on the former, which is now little more than a huge pile of fallen walls.
Present indications show a greater antiquity of the mesa ruin, the site of which afforded more adequate protection. On this supposition the mesa ruins would be considered older than the cliff ruins, and those of the valley the most ancient. If the ruins
in Montezuma valley are the oldest, we can not suppose that the culture originated in the
cliffs and spread to the valley. The circular subterranean kiva bears indication of having
originated in valleys rather than in caverns. Nordenskiöld does not mention the large
ruin on the bluff west of Cliff Palace.

possessed by him, did not hesitate to express decided views on this point:

We are forced to conclude that they [cliff-houses] were abandoned later than the villages on the mesa. Some features, for example, the superposition of walls constructed with the greatest proficiency on others built in a more primitive fashion (see plate XIII) indicate that the cliff-dwellings have been inhabited at two different periods. They were first abandoned, and had partly fallen into ruin, but were subsequently repeopled, new walls being now erected on the ruins of the old. The best explanation hereof seems to be the following: On the plateaux and in the valleys the Pueblo tribes attained their widest distribution and their highest development. The numerous villages at no great distance from each other were strong enough to defy their hostile neighbors. But afterwards, from causes difficult of elucidation, a period of decay set in, the number and population of the villages gradually decreased, and the inhabitants were again compelled to take refuge in the remote fastnesses. Here the people of the Mesa Verde finally succumbed to their enemies. The memory of their last struggle is preserved by the numerous human bones found in many places, strewn among the ruined cliff-dwellings. These human remains occur in situations where it is impossible to assume that they have been interred.

Closely connected with the relative age and the identity of the Mesa Verde cliff-house and pueblo culture are the age and relationship of different cliff-houses of the same region, for example, Cliff Palace and Spruce-tree House. The relative number of kivas may shed light on this point.

The relative proportion of the number of kivas to secular houses varies in Cliff Palace and Spruce-tree House. In the former there are about 7 secular rooms to every kiva; in the latter about 15. Long House has a still more marked difference, there being here only a few secular houses and a maximum number of kivas. Whether this variation has any meaning it is impossible to say definitely; theoretically, as compared with modern pueblos, the proportionately larger number of kivas points to a sociological condition in Cliff Palace characteristic of more primitive times. The larger the number of kivas relatively to secular rooms the older the ruin. Long House would be regarded as older than Cliff Palace, and Cliff Palace older than Spruce-tree House, Balcony House being the most modern and the last of the four to be deserted. A cliff-dwelling with a kiva but without secular rooms is rare, and one with secular rooms but without kivas is likewise unusual. Where the latter exists it is so situated as to indicate that it was subordinated to neighboring large cliff-dwellings.

The relative number of circular kivas in ruins and in modern inhabited pueblos where the circular form of room is found is larger in the ruins than in the inhabited pueblos. The proportionate number of circular rooms to secular rooms in cliff-dwellings of the Mesa Verde is also larger than in pueblo ruins like those of the Chaco. Apparently the older the pueblo the greater the relative number of kivas. If, as is suspected, a larger number of kivas indicates relatively greater age, the explanation may be sought in the amalgamation of clans and the development of religious fraternities. Hypothetically, in early days each clan had its own men's room, or kiva, but when clans were united by marriage and secret ceremonies were no longer limited to individual clans, the participants belonging to several clans, a religious fraternity was developed and several clan kivas consolidated or were enlarged into fraternity kivas such as we find among the Hopi and other Pueblos.

From a study of kivas the conclusion is that Spruce-tree House is more modern than Cliff Palace. This conclusion is borne out also by the fact that the water supply at Spruce-tree House is more abundant than that at Cliff Palace.

In one or two architectural features Cliff Palace is unique, although sharing with other cliff-houses of the Mesa Verde National Park many minor characters. The first difference between Cliff Palace and Spruce-tree House, outside of the disparity in their size and the relatively large proportion of secular to ceremonial rooms in the latter, is the existence in the former of terraces and retaining walls. Spruce-tree House is built on one level, above which rise the secular houses while below are the ceremonial rooms or kivas. The contrast of this simple condition with that of Cliff Palace, with its three terraces and the complicated front wall at several levels thereby necessitated, is apparent.

There are several other ruins in the Mesa Verde Park in which the configuration of the rear of the cave led to the construction of the cliff-house in terrace form. This is well exemplified in the Spring House, where buildings on an upper level occupy much the same relation to those below as the ledge houses to the main ruin, and in ruins in the Canyon de Chelly, like those in Mummy Cave, where this relation of the buildings on the ledge to those on top of the talus is even more pronounced. Architectural features in cliff-houses are due to the geological structure of the cave in which they are situated rather than to cultural differences.

Nothing was found to indicate that Cliff Palace was inhabited during the historic period. The inhabitants were not acquainted with metals brought by white men to the Southwest. The absence of glass and of glazed pottery is also significant. No sheep, horses, or other beasts of burden paid them tribute. In fact, there is no evidence that they had ever heard of white men. These ruins belong to the stone age in America and show no evidence of white man's culture.

Except that it is prehistoric, the period at which Cliff Palace was inhabited is therefore largely a matter for archeological investigation to determine, and thus far no decisive evidence bearing on that point has been produced. It has been held that Cliff Palace is five hundred years old, and some writers have added five centuries to this guess; but the nature of the evidence on which this extreme antiquity is ascribed to the ruin is not warranted by the evidence available.

No additional information was obtained bearing on current theories of the causes that led the ancient occupants of the Mesa Verde cliff-dwellings to adopt this inhospitable and inconvenient habitat. It is probable that one and the same cause led to the abandonment of Spruce-tree House, Cliff Palace, and other Mesa Verde cliff-houses. The inhabitants of these buildings struggled to gain a livelihood against their unfavorable environment until a too-exacting nature finally overcame them. There are no indications that the abandonment of Cliff Palace was cataclysmic in nature: it seems to have been a gradual desertion by one clan after another. One of the primary reasons was change of climate, which caused the water supply to diminish and the crops to fail; but long before its final desertion many clans abandoned the place, and drifting from point to point sought home-sites where water was more abundant. All available data lend weight to a belief that the cliff-houses of Mesa Verde were not abandoned simultaneously, but were deserted one by one. Possibly the inhabitants retired to the river valleys, where water was constant, and later gave up life on the mesa. But even then the culture was not allowed to continue unmodified by outside influences. Where the descendants of Cliff Palace now dwell, or whether they are now extinct, can be determined only by additional research.

Evidence is rapidly accumulating in support of the theory that the " cliff-dweller culture " of our Southwest was preceded by a " pit-house culture," the most prominent feature of which is the small circular or rectangular rooms, artificially excavated laterally in cliffs or vertical in the ground, which served this ancient people either as dwellings or for storage. The side walls of these rooms were supported in some instances by upright logs, and commonly clay was plastered directly on the walls of the excavations. The architectural survival of subterranean rooms exists among the cliff-dwellings in circular underground kivas, the variations of which are so well illustrated in Cliff Palace.

In connection with these " pit rooms," which are never large, may be mentioned the large subterranean artificial excavations found scattered over the Pueblo area of the Southwest. Such occur in the Gila valley, and have been reported from the San Juan drainage; they have been identified as reservoirs and also as kivas. Some of these subterranean rooms are rightly identified as kivas, but others have architectural features that render this interpretation improbable. What their function was and how they are connected with the people who built the smaller subterranean rooms of the Southwest can be determined only by excavations and a study of the features of both types.

The most important step that remains to be taken in the scientific study of the ruins of the Mesa Verde National Park is to discover the relation of the culture of Cliff Palace to that of the neighboring pueblo. This will necessitate the scientific excavation and repair of the latter ruin and a comparison of its major and minor antiquities with those of Cliff Palace. The age of cliff-dwellings in different parts of the Southwest undoubtedly varies. Certain Pueblo ruins are older than some cliff-dwellings, and there are cliff-houses more ancient than Pueblo ruins. Continued research in the Mesa Verde region will doubtless shed light on the relative age of Cliff Palace and the great pueblo ruin opposite it.

○

CLIFF PALACE, FROM THE SPEAKER-CHIEF'S

PHOTOGRAPHED BY F. K. VREELAND

HOUSE TO THE SOUTHERN END

CLIFF PALACE, FROM THE OPPOSITE SIDE OF THE CANYON

THE SOUTHERN END, AFTER AND BEFORE REPAIRING

PHOTOGRAPHED BY F. K. VREELAND

CENTRAL PART, BEFORE REPAIRING

THE ROUND TOWER, FROM THE NORTH

PHOTOGRAPHED BY F. K. VREELAND

GENERAL VIEW OF THE RUIN, BEFORE REPAIRING

CENTRAL PART, AFTER REPAIRING

PHOTOGRAPHED BY R. G. FULLER

SOUTHERN END, AFTER REPAIRING

GROUND PLAN

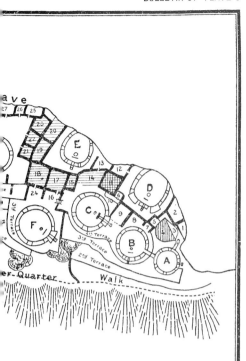

F PALACE

RDE NATIONAL PARK

COLORADO

	2 STORY	3 STORY	4 STORY

John B. Torbert.

FROM SURVEY BY R. G. FULLER

MAIN ENTRANCE

SOUTHERN END, SHOWING REPAIRED TERRACES

TERRACES AT SOUTHERN END, AFTER REPAIRING

TOWER QUARTER, AFTER REPAIRING

TOWER QUARTER

PHOTOGRAPHED BY R. G. FULLER

THE SQUARE TOWER, BEFORE AND AFTER REPAIRING

PHOTOGRAPHED BY R. G. FULLER

b Deflector and flue of kiva

a Third story of square tower, showing dado and decoration

DETAILS OF CLIFF PALACE

SQUARE TOWER, AFTER REPAIRING

OLD QUARTER

SPEAKER-CHIEF'S HOUSE, AFTER REPAIRING

NORTHERN PART, FROM THE SPEAKER-CHIEF'S HOUSE TO THE WESTERN END

PHOTOGRAPHED BY R. G. FULLER

a Tunnel to Kiva B

b Passageway with steps to room 3

DETAILS OF KIVA A

PHOTOGRAPHED BY R. G. FULLER

KIVA H, BEFORE REPAIRING

SOUTHEASTERN WALL OF KIVA Q, BEFORE REPAIRING

PHOTOGRAPHED BY F. K. VREELAND

AX WITH ORIGINAL HANDLE

STONE HATCHETS

a

b   *c*   *d*

STONE OBJECTS

a Pounding stone   *b* Projectile point   *c* Cover for vase   *d* Flat stone slab

a

b   *c*   *d*

e   *f*

VARIOUS OBJECTS FROM CLIFF PALACE

a Pottery fragment with bird-claw decoration in relief   *b, d* Food bowls   *c* Incised stone
e Decorated fragment of earthenware   *f* Cover for vase

FOOD BOWLS

a   b

c   d

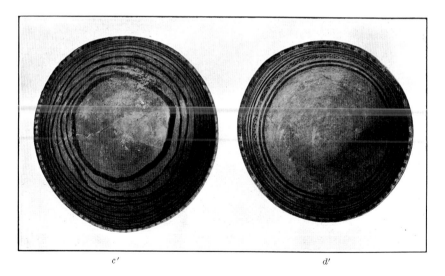

c'   d'

VASES AND FOOD BOWLS

a Mugs from crematory

b Dipper-bowl and corrugated vase

POTTERY

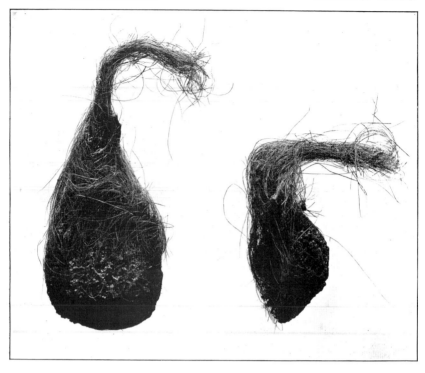

PITCH BALLS AND VASE

a

b

c

RESTS FOR JARS

BASKET HOPPER——SIDE AND BOTTOM VIEWS

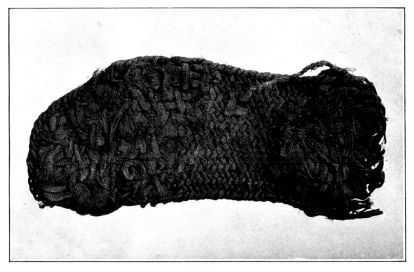

SANDALS

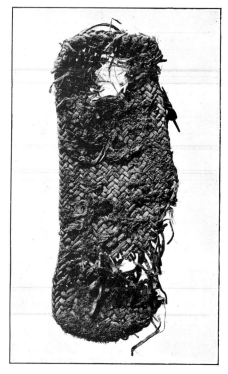

SANDALS

SANDALS

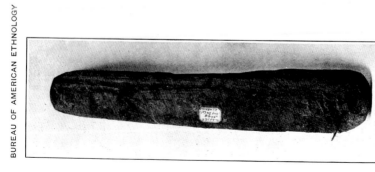

a Billet

b Objects used in game

c Billet

WOODEN OBJECTS

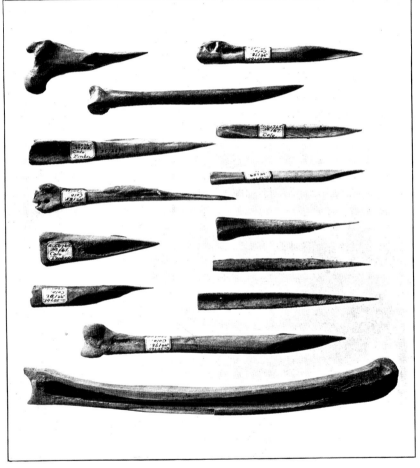

BONE IMPLEMENTS

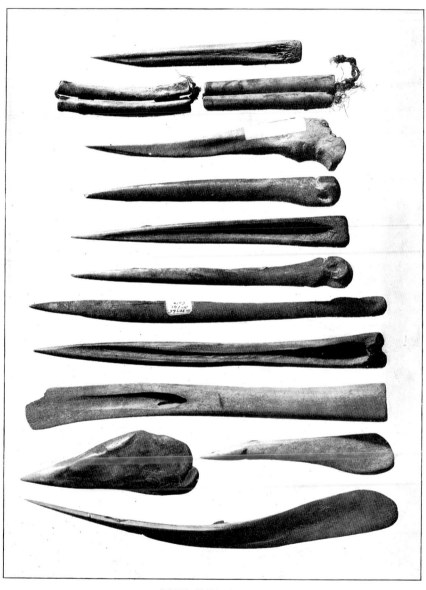

BONE IMPLEMENTS